Theology Without Boundaries

Other Books by Carnegie Samuel Calian

Today's Pastor in Tomorrow's World

The Significance of Eschatology in the Thoughts of
Nicholas Berdyaev

Berdyaev's Philosophy of Hope (revised edition)

Icon and Pulpit: The Protestant-Orthodox Encounter

Grace, Guts and Goods: How to Stay Christian in an
Affluent Society

The Gospel According to the Wall Street Journal

For All Your Seasons: Biblical Directions Through Life's Passages

Where's the Passion for Excellence in the Church?

Theology Without Boundaries

Encounters of
Eastern Orthodoxy
and Western Tradition

CARNEGIE SAMUEL CALIAN

WESTMINSTER/JOHN KNOX PRESS
Louisville, Kentucky

Book design by Publishers' WorkGroup

First edition

Published by Westminster/John Knox Press
Louisville, Kentucky

This book is printed on acid-free paper that meets the American National Standards Institute Z39.48 standard. ∞

PRINTED IN THE UNITED STATES OF AMERICA

9 8 7 6 5 4 3 2 1

Library of Congress Cataloging-in-Publication Data

Calian, Carnegie Samuel.
   Theology without boundaries : encounters of Eastern Orthodoxy and Western tradition / Carnegie Samuel Calian. — 1st ed.
        p.   cm.
   Includes bibliographical references and index.
   ISBN 0-664-25156-0

   1. Orthodox Eastern Church—Doctrines.   2. Orthodox Eastern Church—Relations.   3. Christian union.   I. Title.
BX320.2.C32 1992
281.9—dc20   91-32972

Dedicated with love
to
Grace Ajemian Zobian

Contents

Acknowledgments

This volume has been a long time in the making. Many lessons have been learned since Westminster Press published *Icon and Pulpit* (1968) during the editorship of Roland Tapp. Discussions and encounters have transpired, greater understanding and maturity have been reached, and yet unresolved issues still exist. The ecumenical dialogue continues, and it provides the impetus for this volume.

My special thanks to editors Davis Perkins and Harold Twiss of Westminster/John Knox Press for their encouragement and support. My appreciation also to publisher Robert McIntyre and the entire staff for the support I have seen with this publication and four of my previous books.

I want to express heartfelt thanks to Linda Smith, my secretary, for preparing the manuscript, and to Doris Zobian Calian, my marriage partner of thirty-two years, for editing assistance and loving criticism. My appreciation to Alida Clark, a former student and doctoral candidate at the University of Pittsburgh, for bibliographical and technical assistance, and to the staff of Barbour Library at Pittsburgh Theological Seminary for their cheerful and supportive help in providing research materials. Thanks also to Charles De Mirjian for his suggestions and encouragement. The dedication is a tribute to a courageous Christian mother who bridged both Eastern and Western Christendom and at eighty-six years of age approaches each day in faith and thanksgiving.

Finally, a long overdue word of grateful appreciation to colleagues past and present who have provided stimuli and opportunities for clarifying my thoughts. I am especially grateful to the editors of journals such as *Theology Today, The Greek Orthodox Theological Review, Sobornost, Reformed World, Journal of Ecumenical Studies, Ecumenical Review, Worldview,* and others who have given me opportunity through their pages to

ACKNOWLEDGMENTS

express and articulate my thoughts and findings. As a pilgrim scholar, I am well aware that none of us travels alone in our journey of discovery and dialogue—research and teaching have always been cooperative ventures for me. Nevertheless, I take sole responsibility for the materials in this volume and pray that its contents might be to the glory of God.

Preface

Through the centuries, Eastern Orthodoxy has maintained its tradition in spite of opposition and immeasurable suffering. The Eastern church has faced many challenges and has suffered considerably, but it continues to survive and bear witness to its rich heritage. The following chapters are not a systematic discussion of these challenges, but rather an attempt to highlight some of the inherent issues vital to Christians of all traditions who are drawn closer together today through the will for unity.

These pages seek to widen our horizons beyond a solely Western or Eastern orientation of the Christian faith. Many in the West have been turning eastward for fresh forms of spirituality and renewal. This has led to a resurgence of interest in Eastern religions in recent years. This exploration has largely neglected the Eastern dimension within Christianity. Actually, Christianity is also an Eastern religion. Yet the majority of Western Christians neglect Eastern origins. Taking these facts into account, this book seeks areas of creative convergence and exchange between Christians East and West. In a larger sense, the book seeks to make Christians more globally alive to the breadth and diversity of our faith, forcing each of us out of parochial tracks and ethnic enclaves.

As Christians around the world reach out to one another, the possibility exists for a new spirituality to emerge from the roots of yesterday's diverse traditions and perspectives. We have seen this new bond of unity developing already as the liberation theology from South America finds a responsive chord in the Northern Hemisphere. In a similar way, an unfolding of Eastern Christian theology and spirituality can become an enriching and liberating experience, renewing bonds of faith and commitment in the West. Whether we turn East or West, every Christian is undeniably involved in a process of becoming spiritually unified under one Lord. An underlying conviction throughout the pages of this volume is the work of the Holy Spirit in bringing us together.

Today, the unfortunate fact remains that in the West, Eastern Christianity remains largely undiscovered among our colleges, universities, seminaries, and churches. Very few courses on Eastern Christianity are actively offered today in academic and theological centers. The influence of Eastern Christianity must no longer be limited to ethnic enclaves and occasional ecumenical gatherings. We must make a conscious effort to easternize the Christian faith once again. This book is designed as a step in that direction, seeking to promote greater dialogue and exchange among Christians of the East and West.

Christianity, in seeking to overcome its own walls, borders, and fences, is still confronted with unresolved tensions from the past. These historical and theological discussions from the past contain important lessons for today. Questions must be raised concerning which councils are ecumenical, the value of confessions in an age of ecumenism, the interrelationship of revelation and history, the need for a theology of spirituality, and the source of authority for all Christians. We are faced also with challenges from without, such as the contemporary meaning of God, the influence of Marxism, and the secularization of Christian eschatology. Collectively, these issues present an awesome global agenda for Christians within a shrinking world.

Today all Christians confess the historicity of their faith as well as the boundless nature of God's gracious Spirit, which transcends historical limitations. The interaction between history and the Spirit confronts the believer in every age. The lives of Cyril Lucaris and Nikos Kazantzakis are cases in point. The current emphasis upon biography as theology is vividly captured in the lives of these two figures. The gift of our time is to unfold their life stories as an ecumenical community living in the new context of village Christianity—the international dimensions of diversity and human resources have yet to be fully discovered. Working together *in* community, each household of faith can bring its insights and contributions to bear upon the crucial problems facing us.

The twentieth century has seen ecumenism come of age. Looking to the future, will this ecumenical drive decline? Are we already in a postecumenical climate? Many current observers would answer yes. From the longer perspective, however, the answer is definitely no. Ecumenical cooperation will increase rather than decline in the years ahead. Ecumenism may take unanticipated turns and forms, but to fight it or pretend it does not exist is to be asleep to the tremendous forces calling for unity. The future of Christians depends on sharing one another's ecclesiastical treasures and removing barriers to greater freedom of movement. To go beyond cultural boundaries may create some confusion at first, but the benefits and fresh perspectives to be gained within the wider household of faith are too great to be ignored.

As ecumenism, more global than ever, pushes us closer together, there will be added opportunities for discussion with a wide cross-section of persons from varied backgrounds. Ecumenism has become a staple today encouraged by our technological advances. Whether it will be a healthy or sick ecumenism will be largely determined by the participants, professional and novice alike, and the quality of dialogue that takes place.

Care must be taken as we acknowledge the pluralism existing in the world lest we succumb to a superficial form of tolerance. Superficial congeniality will be detrimental to everyone's tradition. An eclectic stance can only result in a tossed-salad type of ecumenism without direction. Each person's task is clear in the coming days; each of us must examine why we believe the way we do as we take a closer look at our own religious habits.

A cloud of promise and storm hovering over our ecumenical plateau represents the current situation. All future discussion of historical and theological questions will transcend geographical considerations such as East, West, North, and South. We are living in an *ecumenopolis* technologically, if not theologically. The twenty-first century promises to take the ecumenical movement beyond the beginnings of adulthood to maturity.

In this unfolding process, the chapters of this book serve as a pilgrim's map to issues and concerns that are vital if Christians are to engage creatively with one another in tomorrow's world. Suggestions and insights will be offered for a *theology without boundaries* evolving within our international Christian village. Written in a spirit of ecumenical hope, these issue-oriented themes express the conviction that our destiny is bright if our present engagements are characterized by honest realism.

PART ONE

EASTERN ORTHODOXY AND THE SPIRIT OF RENEWAL

1

Ecumenical Councils and the Spirit

One of the puzzling problems confronting contemporary Christians is the question of ecumenical councils. This is especially important to Orthodoxy, which emphasizes the historic authority of councils. Which councils in the church's history are ecumenical? Vatican II and the World Council of Churches, as well as the important confessional conferences within Orthodoxy and Protestantism, highlight with theological urgency this question.

The World Council of Churches Commission on Faith and Order has studied the significance of the councils of the early church for the ecumenical movement.[1] The study addressed questions such as "(a) How were the Councils convened; what was their membership; how was the consensus formed at the Council; to what authorities did the Councils appeal as normative? (b) Did the resolutions of the Councils have validity in themselves, or did this depend on their reception in the churches? (c) How did the word 'ecumenical' come into use in relation to the Councils?"[2] Our present discussion will pursue these topics in the following manner: first, with consideration of the priority of the Council of Nicaea; second, with a brief survey of the councils and issues to Vatican II; and last, toward a theology of councils for the future.

Before we proceed, we must define our understanding of "ecumenical." The term "ecumenical" has had a venerable history in Christendom.[3] "Ecumenical" (*oikoumene*) in its biblical usage connotes an inclusiveness of both space (the whole inhabited earth) and time (the history of Israel and the nations of the world). The true ecumenical context in scripture unites space and time eschatologically (Ps. 24 [*cf.* Septuagint Ps. 23:1] and Heb. 2:5) when the Lord of history will fellowship with the whole inhabited earth. From this eschatological perspective all ecclesiastical councils of whatever tradition are at best *pre-ecumenical*, signs pointing to what God has in store for a redeemed humanity. Our use of "ecumenical" in this study, however, is limited to Christians, and thus the *oikoumene* refers to the Christian *koinonia* (fellowship) throughout the inhabited earth. It should be kept in mind that *oikoumene* in its biblical setting is universal, missionary, and eschatological in uniting both space and time; thus it addresses itself to the totality of humanity past, present, and future.

The Priority of Nicaea

Church councils had precedent long before the Council of Nicaea (A.D. 325); in fact, the origin of church councils is said to be the meeting in Jerusalem (Acts 15; Gal. 2) traditionally referred to as the "Apostolic Council."[4] The reason for the preeminence in Christendom enjoyed by the Council of Nicaea is the set of factors that had previously never converged in the church's history. These factors give Nicaea an *ecumenical character.*

Emperor Constantine took the initiative for calling this unique council. According to Georg Kretschmar, the churchmen who gathered at Nicaea "were apparently able to embrace in one harmonious vision the universality of the empire and of the church and to regard the emperor's ecumenical gathering as a renewal of the miracle of Pentecost."[5] Nicaea was not a council of the East nor of the West, but symbolized the totality of Christendom at that time. "Even the Persian church of the Sassanid Empire received the decisions of the council. To the present day the 'faith of Nicaea' continues to function as a bond of union for the large Christian churches."[6] The Nicene Creed,[7] for example, continues to be uttered in all the major traditions of Christendom, exemplifying this common bond of unity (with the important exception of the *filioque* clause, which appears only in the Western version of the creed[8]).

The ecumenical factors of universality and authority seen in Constantine's desire to hold a council were exceeded only by the prevailing wish of that time to establish unity both politically and ecclesiastically. Constantine viewed political and ecclesiastical unity as interdependent. The possibility of unity was threatened at the time by Arius and his followers.[9] It was Constantine's hope to establish a unifying bond among the feuding churchmen and thereby create the semblance of a state church. The fact that Constantine did not achieve his goal is reflected in the subsequent councils. For Constantine, the aim of the council was not that of expulsion (in this case, of the Arians in their unorthodox teachings), but rather to set forth the truth in a spirit of unity among the assembled clergy and laity at Nicaea. Kretschmar writes,

> It was Constantine's desire to crown the great work of pacification by readmitting, after a suitable period of time, the Arians who had been excluded in 325. The synod, or a committee of the synod, presumably reassembled in 327, declared Arius' most recent and quite obscure confession to be orthodox, and resolved that he be reconciled to the church. The emperor lifted the order of banishment. But the successor of Bishop Alexander of Alexandria, Athanasius, who had taken part in the Council of Nicaea as a deacon, did not accept this decision. With this refusal begins a new phase of the trinitarian controversy, the struggle over the proper understanding of Nicaea.[10]

In short, the Council of Nicaea expressed ecumenical qualities of universality and authority but did not restore unity to the church.

The Council of Nicaea also introduced catholicity. The concept of catholicity implies far more than geographical universality; it points to the qualitative spirit of unity symbolized by the gathering. Catholicity also refers to the dogmatic presuppositions underlying the life of the church. The question of truth and faithfulness to the gospel, then, is at stake under the category of catholicity. The aim of the council was to protect the truth of the gospel. Thus the council set forth a *necessarium* of Christian belief without presenting a compendium of theological truths. The council sought to emphasize the fundamental truth inherent in the gospel, with scripture as the essential guideline to the apostolic mind.

It is important to note here that most of the early councils met after the canon was closed. The Council fathers considered themselves subject to the scriptures as their norm.[11] The Council of Nicaea also sought to establish this quality of catholicity (and apostolicity) centered in the gospel and perpetuated by the canon and tradition. From the standpoint of catholicity, then, Nicaea was more than a conference; it was a confrontation and directive to be obedient to the truth—it can be interpreted as being faithful to the spirit of the emerging canon. Those at Nicaea were desirous of expressing the truth (or dogma) of the gospel in a binding way. The Council of Nicaea thus delineated theologically the meaning of catholicity for the Christendom of that day.

In addition to the ecumenical dimension of catholicity, universality, authority, and unity, the Council of Nicaea enjoyed almost immediate *reception* by Christians throughout the land. Reception by the laity is an important criterion for the ecumenicity of a council. This concept of reception is especially important from the Orthodox viewpoint. For the Orthodox, the legitimacy of a council is dependent on the response of the laity. According to Emilianos of Meloa,

> The laity, which constitutes the bulk of the body of Christ, constantly collaborates with the clergy in the task of defending and teaching dogma and tradition. Since a universal council is the visible instrument of the tradition, it must be aware of the feelings of the people, who are responsible for putting the canons into effect. Church history shows that a council may fail to be recognized as ecumenical when it fails to become part of the conscience of the people, for the people must acknowledge it and make its provisions their own. The supreme organ of infallibility is therefore the entire body of Christ, as soon as the people embrace the pronouncements of the council.[12]

Reception by the people of God (*laos*) in actuality is the act of synthesizing universality and catholicity.

In practice, the reception of a council like Nicaea is a spiritual process that contains by its very nature a degree of openness. It is subject to the leading of the Holy Spirit. From the viewpoint of those attending the council, it is the pneumatic centeredness rather than the imperial injunction which serves as the theological basis for the council's authority. The delegates at the council "understood themselves increasingly as an instrument of the Holy Spirit, as a voice which therefore must be heard."[13] Reception by the *whole church* gave the council its ecumenical recognition, as in the case of Nicaea. Reception, then, is not something added externally to the inner pneumatic authority of council, but rather, reception confirms it. An ecumenical council, in other words, "is a council which has been recognized by the church scattered throughout the world."[14]

Finally, let us consider the criteria for the reception of a council, especially with regard to dogmatic decisions. The test of reception is whether or not the council held fast to the ancient apostolic tradition against new heresies, as in the case of the Arians at Nicaea. The Orthodox are quite adamant on this point. For the Orthodox, "the ecumenicity of a council is determined neither by the number of participating bishops, nor by the subsequent confirmation of the bishops of Rome as Catholics claim. There is only an internal criterion: the teaching must be in absolute harmony with what the church has always believed and taught."[15] Admittedly, nontheological factors are involved in the entire conciliar process including reception, but ultimately reception is a spiritual process that affirms the apostolic tradition. Proof of its spirituality, the Faith and Order Commission reported, lies precisely in "the long process of critical appropriation which both preceded the formal reception and followed it. Reception as a spiritual event corresponds to the council's claim to be the voice of the Holy Spirit. This presupposes that the same spirit of God who leads to all truth by witnessing to Jesus, the incarnate Word of God, is at work both in the council and the church as a whole."[16] Thus, the factor of reception is not to be taken lightly when considering the reasons behind the priority given to the Council of Nicaea as the prototype of an ecumenical council. The Christian church had shifted considerably in its global status from the modest beginnings of the initial apostolic gathering in Jerusalem.

Councils and Issues
to Vatican II

We have already mentioned the Arian controversy that surrounded the Council of Nicaea; this was followed by many additional issues considered in subsequent councils. Not all the issues or councils will be dealt with here, but a sufficient number will be considered to indicate the contemporary ambiguity that permeates the status of ecumenical councils from both Eastern and Western viewpoints.

Following the Council of Nicaea, the succeeding councils defined and clarified the dogma of the church, resulting (for good or ill) in the further fragmentation of the *Corpus Christianum*. The criteria for the ecumenicity and acceptance of any particular council were not universally shared by all those in Christendom. The Arians were finally severed from the wider fellowship of Christians at the Second Ecumenical Council of Constantinople in A.D. 381. The Nestorians were ousted following the Third Ecumenical Council at Ephesus in A.D. 431. The Oriental Orthodox churches (sometimes incorrectly called "monophysites") were alienated at the Fourth Ecumenical Council of Chalcedon in A.D. 451. The fifth and sixth ecumenical councils at Constantinople (A.D. 553 and 680–1 respectively) stand in the shadow of Chalcedon, further defining Christology and condemning aspects of Nestorianism and monophysitism in its related form of monotheletism. The Seventh Ecumenical Council at Nicaea in A.D. 787 is the last council of an "ecumenical stature," from the viewpoint of Byzantine Orthodoxy. It concerned itself with the problem of iconoclasm and declared itself strongly in favor of the veneration of images (icons). Latin Christendom (the Roman Church) continued to take the initiative in holding ecumenical councils, numbering them consecutively from the first seven, until we recently arrived at the twenty-first ecumenical council, better known to the world as Vatican II. From this cursory survey, the evident fragmentation of the *Corpus Christianum* from a conciliar viewpoint can be sharply seen.

It can be quickly surmised that the ecumenical councils were perhaps a greater source of division than of unity. Such a surface appraisal would be incorrect. In what sense, then, can these councils be regarded as ecumenical, having a universal validity for all of Christendom? It appears that ecumenical councils have become identified with the practice of exclusion, resulting in a fragmented Christendom that produced a kind of regionalism, with Byzantine, Oriental, and Latin leanings. Each region ("region" implying a common sharing of theological content rather than a geographic area) does not share the ecumenicity of the others in its entirety. This factor adds to the ambiguity and confusion surrounding the question of councils.

For example, one criterion for the ecumenicity of a council in the Latin ecclesiastical world is that the power to summon an ecumenical council resides with the pope. In the Greek East, such authority has resided with the state. In practice, however, such theological orientations of papal and imperial authority are much more complex. According to Georg Kretschmar, while all the early councils were indeed called by emperors, this factor does not explain why other synods or councils called by emperors during the same period were later rejected, "such as those of 449 and 754, or the Second Trullan Council, which specifically described itself as ecumenical but which was recognized only in the East. On the other hand, the council of 381, which was not attended by representatives of the West, was nevertheless recognized by the West later, while the papal synod of Martin I (649) did not attain recognition."[17] The regional orientations of the Greek East (imperial) and Latin West (papal) influence and compound the confusion regarding the necessary bases upon which councils are considered ecumenical.

For instance, Francis Dvornik, the distinguished Roman Catholic scholar on Byzantine Orthodoxy, has studied the validity of the so-called Eighth Ecumenical Council (869–70), the last ecumenical council to be held in the East. This council concerned itself with the controversy of Photius, Patriarch of Constantinople, in his struggle with the papacy. The culmination of the struggle was the condemnation of the Patriarch Photius as a usurper of the patriarchal throne of Constantinople, and the reinstatement of Saint Ignatius in his stead at the Synod of 869–70. This council was later added to the seven ecumenical councils and called the Eighth Ecumenical Council by the Roman Church. "This Council called itself ecumenical," Dvornik says,

> because it was convoked by an Emperor—Basil I—as were all previous ecumenical councils. The invitations to assist at it were addressed to the bishops of the Empire and it was attended by the representative of Pope Hadrian II and four other Patriarchs. In spite of this it was opened in the presence of only twelve bishops, and its Acts were signed by only the one hundred and ten Fathers who had responded to the repeated exhortations of the Emperor to appear at its session. The reason for this meagre attendance was that the great majority of Byzantine prelates considered the accusations launched against Photius as unjust, since he had been canonically elected by a local synod after the resignation of Ignatius in 856. Because the majority of the clergy had ignored the decisions of this Council, Ignatius had difficulties in the administration of his patriarchate. Fortunately, this situation was cleared up when the Emperor brought Photius back from exile and entrusted him with the education of his sons. Then both Ignatius and Photius were reconciled.[18]

This was not the end of the episode. The Byzantine Church needed healing within itself and also reconciliation with the papacy.

Another council was planned for the purpose of reconciliation on all sides. The Emperor and Ignatius asked Pope John VIII to send his representatives, but Ignatius died before the papal representatives reached Constantinople. Photius was reinstated as Patriarch. "The Council took place in November of 879 and ended in March, 880. Photius was reinstated by the numerous conciliar Fathers with the assent of the papal legates and the representatives of the other Patriarchs. The Council of 869–870 which had condemned Photius and his followers was abrogated."[19] Why, then, does the Roman church continue to this day to count a council that has been abrogated as ecumenical? This is an embarrassing question for Dvornik in his quest for truth and for cordiality with Byzantine Orthodoxy. Acquaintance with Orthodoxy would inform any Western observer, Protestant or Roman Catholic, that Orthodoxy gives great honor to the first seven ecumenical councils. Orthodoxy considers itself as the Church of the Councils.[20] Greek Uniates tried unsuccessfully to designate as the Eighth Ecumenical Council the Council of Lyons (1274); having failed, they tried later to do the same with the Council of Ferrara-Florence (1438–39).

How then did the Western church come to abandon this earlier tradition of seven ecumenical councils, which it shared with Byzantine Orthodoxy, by adding the synod (or council) of 869–70 as the Eighth Ecumenical Council, which subsequent history invalidated? Dvornik suggests that the recognition by the Roman church of the Ignatian Council as the Eighth Ecumenical Council was due to the influence of a hidden agenda during the reign of Pope Gregory VII,

> who opened the Lateran archives to his canonists who were looking for new arguments for the papal primacy and who were against the intervention of laymen in the appointment of bishops and abbots. They needed a strongly worded official document which they could use in their fight against the investiture, or appointment of clergy to ecclesiastical dignities by influential laymen. They found such a document in Canon twenty-two voted by the Ignatian Council, which forbade laymen to influence the appointment of prelates.[21]

It should be recalled that Photius had unusual power in his lay status prior to his rapid rise into the clerical hierarchy.

Such power in the laity was a threat to the papacy and its sovereignty in the choice of prelates. Gregorian canonists and reformers used Canon Twenty-two as their strongest argument for freedom in the election of prelates. "To give more weight to this argument," Dvornik says, "they promoted the Ignatian Council to one of the most important ecumenical synods, overlooking the Acts of the Photian Council which had cancelled the Council of 869–70, although the Acts of this council were also kept in the Lateran Archives."[22] In short, it appears that Roman canonists found this council an effective weapon in their struggle to strengthen the papacy. Thus the council of 869–70, which had been canceled, began to be numbered again among the ecumenical councils as the Eighth Council at the end of the eleventh and the beginning of the twelfth centuries.

Dvornik has done us a service in tracing the strange development leading to the acceptance of the Ignatian Council of 869–70 as an ecumenical council, despite the fact that nothing is known of any official decree in the life of the Roman church giving the status "ecumenical" to the council. Dvornik concludes that a seemingly extraordinary oversight on the part of the eleventh-century canonists led to the elevation of the Ignatian Council into the Eighth Ecumenical Council. From the Roman standpoint, this clearly illustrates that the East and West were in perfect accord regarding the numbering of the councils until the twelfth century.

Turning from the Orthodox-Catholic dialogue on the numbering of the ecumenical councils, there is a parallel discussion and debate over the ecumenicity of the Council of Trent between Protestants and Catholics. The Council of Trent (1545–63) is regarded as the nineteenth ecumenical council by the Roman church. Trent issued many doctrinal and disciplinary decrees as a corrective to the Protestant Reformation. The Roman canonists at the time were interested in seeing that the documents issued from Trent would receive ecumenical status. Strengthening the papacy against the spirit of conciliarism that Protestants and Orthodox favored was another motivation behind Trent, even though the papacy had already triumphed over the conciliarist attempts at the councils of Basel, Ferrara, and Florence (1431–42). Today, the speculative question has been raised: If the conciliar spirit had prevailed in the Roman church, would further fragmentation within Western Christendom have been avoided?

Hubert Jedin, in his scholarly study on the ecumenical councils, has suggested that there was only one way to counteract the further disintegration of Western Christendom and that was to hold a council during the decisive years of the Reformation (1521–1525). As early as 1524, the emperor Charles V significantly proposed the convocation of a general council in the little town of Trent, but Pope Clement VII was opposed at that time to holding any council. Such are the ironies of history! Peter Meinhold writes,

> It is indeed hard to visualize the course of the reformation that would have ensued if a council had actually been held during those years. It may be that there would have been bitter controversy between the council and Luther, who had declared at Worms that he could not believe in "councils alone" inasmuch as they did not represent a unanimous tradition. But it is equally probable that the convening of a council in those years of decision would have prevented the final rupture of Western Christendom, and the outbreak of the Peasants' War and other radical reform movements might have been made impossible. It is likely that a council held at so early a date would have been in a position to prevent the struggles that actually took place later by clarifying such questions as the proper relationships between papal and episcopal power and between the spiritual authority of the church and the actual administrative power of its highest tribunals.[23]

In the end, the spirit of suspicion rather than conciliarity had its sway in the papacy.

In spite of the outcome, the Reformers continued to advocate a conciliar approach, placing great emphasis upon the first four councils and subjecting all conciliar pronouncements to the testimony of scripture. Luther and Calvin viewed the distinguishing characteristic of conciliarism as the idea of an *ecclesia repraesentativa*. They saw it as the community of believers meeting together in mutual harmony. Their views were very similar to the Orthodox view of *sobornost'* (a fraternal fellowship in unity). For the Reformers, all the people of God should be represented in the council—bishops, priests, and laity. Peter Meinhold asserts that the distinguishing feature of conciliarism

> is that the church is understood as the community of believers. The authority inherent in the church is exercised through the council where all believers are represented, partly by their bishops and clergy, partly by the laity present. Thus the general council appears as representative of the fulness of spiritual power resident in the church as a whole. Hence the council has the right to judge the pope: it can fill the papal office, even in matters of dogma its teaching authority is superior to that of the pope.[24]

Of course, conciliarism interpreted in these terms was opposed to the papacy and the Council of Trent in the latter's subordinate relationship to the pope. The Reformers therefore refused the extended invitation to attend the council. The absence of the Protestants, however, did not deter the Roman canonists from adding Trent to the list of ecumenical councils. In actuality the ecumenicity of the Council of Trent sought opposition rather than reconciliation; it became known as the Council of the Counter-Reformation. Not until the Second Vatican Council (for the First Vatican Council was but a further extension of the dogmatic labors of Trent), the twenty-first ecumenical council for the Roman church, has the climate been set for Protestants, Orthodox, and Catholics to strive together toward constructing a mutually shared theology for future ecumenical councils.

Toward a Pneumatic Theology of Councils

It is evident that no official list of recognized ecumenical councils will be satisfying to all church traditions in the East or the West. We can count as many as twenty-one councils if we are Roman Catholics and zero if we are contemporary Arians, with an interesting and varying range of two for Nestorians, three for the Oriental Orthodox, four for the Reformers, and seven for the Byzantine Orthodox.[25] Also, note that the ante-Nicene synods were called by bishops of local churches without the functionary aid of the state. In fact, the Council of Nicaea summoned by Constantine constituted in itself an innovation. This observation does not take away from the significance of Nicaea but rather should highlight in our search for a theology of councils that the early church in the first three decisive centuries of the church actually managed without "ecumenical councils" (this fact should humble any Christian tradition claiming ecumenicity for a council). Finally, let it be said that the Council of Jerusalem (Acts 15:1–29), which served later as the primitive proto-type for Nicaea, announced its decisions in a pneumatic spirit: "For it has seemed good to the Holy Spirit and to us . . ." (v. 28). These remarks should be kept in mind along with the characteristics of universality, unity, and catholicity noted in reference to the Council of Nicaea as we move toward a theology of councils for the future.

A realistic ecumenism looking to the future will not be satisfied with less than an ecumenical council that can be shared by the entire *oik-oumene* of Christians. The Council of Nicaea came the closest to achiev-ing this goal, and hence its honorary priority in all quarters of the Christians' *oikoumene*. The Second Vatican Council in the 1960s pro-claimed itself from a Roman standpoint to be "ecumenical." However, almost one-half of the Christian *oikoumene* could not officially *vote* in its proceedings (in spite of considerable influence that Protestant and Or-thodox *observers* had upon the council). "In reality, therefore," according to Roman Catholic theologian Hans Küng, Vatican II "is not an ecu-menical council, but a Roman Catholic council."[26] Given this awareness, Küng rightly surmised that the full factual ecumenical credibility of a council in the future

> cannot be established by theoretical arguments, but only by the reunion of separated Christians. This can be achieved only if a future council should again really represent the whole *oikumene* and gain the recognition of the whole *oikumene*. It may take a long, an unbearably long time, before this comes to pass. But what is decisive today is that the first step has been taken in this direction. By the epoch-making fact of orienting the Second Vatican Council toward the goal of reunion, John XXIII has not only aroused great hopes; he has also greatly strengthened the ecumenical credibleness of this council.[27]

Keeping this cautionary note of realism in mind lest we become ecu-menically impatient with one another, let us proceed to give two neces-sary theological criteria or categories that must be seriously considered in planning a council in the future.

The first is the theological criterion of *reception*. Reception (we have already noted) is an open-ended process and not subject to any rigid procedure. By reception, according to the Faith and Order commission's report, we imply the process by which churches and their traditions "accept the decision of a council and thereby recognize its authority. Such reception refers only to the conciliar decisions and does not nec-essarily include a position toward the proceedings during the council by which they came into being. Naturally, however, a refusal of reception can be based on the judgment that the council was illegal or, especially, that it did not hold to the norms of preserving apostolic tradition."[28] From the standpoint of the *oikoumene,* an ecumenical council is one that has been received and recognized by Christian churches wherever they exist.

Reception implies more than mathematical unanimity; it may even reside with a minority, but above all it centers on a common search for the mind of the spirit. Reception is a spiritual process under the sovereignty of the Holy Spirit, the universal bishop of the *oikoumene.* An ecumenical council, according to Hans Küng, "is not a democratic parliament in which it is merely a matter of producing a majority, even a slim one, for or against a decision. Rather, an ecumenical council is the representation of the Church and of her unity, which can be credibly expressed only in the unanimity of decisions effected by the Spirit. It is not in the large 'faction' that the Holy Spirit of unity manifests His presence but in the concord of all."[29] Reception points above all to a pneumatic consensus among the Christian churches.

A pneumatic consensus must be achieved sooner or later if an ecumenical council in the future is to be authoritative for the *oikoumene.* The lack of such consensus, writes Yves Congar,

> would then be a sign that the council does not represent the ecumenical Church in her fullness. Unanimity and fellowship are the work of the Holy Spirit (see II Cor. 13:13, *koinonia*). In order to grasp the deeper meaning of councils we must take into consideration the Holy Spirit as a decisive personage. Councils always call themselves assemblies in the Holy Spirit at which Christ invisibly presides (sometimes this presence of Christ is concretely represented by a picture of Christ or by Holy Scripture, which lies open on an altar). The passage in Matthew (18:20), which holds out the promise of the presence of the Lord wherever the Church is gathered in harmony and in community, is always quoted.

Thus time and again what the first Christian testimony states about the councils of the Church must always be realized anew. Tertullian writes, ". . . the representation of the whole of Christendom is celebrated with great veneration. How worthy of a guiding faith that this council be gathered from all places for Christ! Behold, how good and joyful it is when brethren dwell together!"[30] This, then, is the first necessary theological criterion for a future ecumenical council: reception by means of a pneumatic consensus.

The second of these suggested twofold theological criteria is the need for *continuity*. Reception by means of a pneumatic consensus will always keep the door open for change under the leading of the Spirit, but there is also the task of discerning the spirits, hence the theological requirement for continuity. The criterion for continuity is an acknowledgment that any future ecumenical council must be biblical in content and apostolic in character. Anything less than this would not have the quality of catholicity to merit the distinction of being known as an ecumenical council by the churches.

Within the very nature of a council, there will exist a constant tension between continuity and change, between reception and revelation, as the churches search for the mind of Christ in their day. The inevitable tension is actually an essential function of an ecumenical council. The tension implies that the council constitutes the ecclesiastical authority to correctly interpret scripture and tradition; at the same time the council itself is also subject to the authority of scripture and tradition. It is precisely at this point that the Council of Nicaea serves as the most creative model for an ecumenical council of the people of God. There, according to Küng,

> matters were not to be settled by some kind of scholarly predilections and political tendencies, nor by any kind of fanciful philosophy or fanciful theology, nor by any kind of scholastic theses or scholastic systems, nor by any national university or monastic tradition, but by the word of God in the holy writings of the Old and New Testaments. Can what Athanasius said about the Fathers of Nicaea "breaking Holy Scripture" be said about the Fathers of *all* councils? We cannot overlook the fact that the closeness to Scripture of individual councils has been very different. There was a great difference between Nicaea, where it was primarily a question of the interpretation of Scripture, and the later post-Chalcedon councils where it was often primarily a question of seeing who could forge the longest chain of proofs for his argument, made up of quotations from the Fathers.[31]

As in the case of Nicaea, any future ecumenical council must also take the *responsible risk* of reinterpreting the truth inherent in the biblical revelation and transmitted through the respective Christian traditions. These truths must then be placed into the idioms of tomorrow's *laos*.

Use of these theological criteria will provide valuable guidelines to future ecumenical councils in which all Christian churches may participate. When the criteria of reception by means of a pneumatic consensus and of continuity by means of scripture and tradition are made to converge with each other, the result will be a creative tension through which the churches will have the opportunity to discern more clearly the bidding of the Spirit.

The pneumatic consensus sought through councils brings our attention to an even more encompassing question—can we discern the working of the Spirit through the historical process? Is our spirituality and theologizing taking place in a world governed by God's Spirit? Is there any spiritual activity occurring outside ourselves—in the very events of human history? These questions, among others, will be the subjects of the following chapter, which examines the attempts of East and West to probe for a pneumatic consensus of divine involvement in secular history.

2

Holy Spirit and the Historical Process

Divine intervention through the Holy Spirit within human history was illustrated by two early Christian designations for Sunday. Among the faithful, the first day of the week became known as the Eighth Day and the Lord's Day. These two Christian names for Sunday were derived from the liturgical actions of baptism and the Lord's Supper. The use of these titles by the earliest Christians sums up the significance of Sunday as the beginning of a new aeon. Every Sunday celebrated since that time bears witness to God's revelation in Jesus Christ.

Sunday points not only to redemptive history; it also emphasizes God's revelation at creation. As the first day of the week, Sunday is a "symbol of the creation of the world and so the symbol of the beginning of all things: at the same time, it was the day following the sabbath, the 'eighth day' and a symbol of the new aeon without end."[1] Hence for the confessing Christians, creation and redemption converge significantly on the Eighth Day. The Greek Fathers were aware of this organic link between creation and redemption; for them the Eighth Day or "age" leads creation into eternity.[2] Therefore, we can speak of an eschatological orientation that begins at creation, and not with the advent (incarnation) of Jesus Christ. Creation, redemption, and the *eschaton* are all related within the mystery of the triune God.

Between Dogmatism and Despair

Historians and theologians, as historic beings in time and space, cannot escape the responsibility to find meaning in life. Such meaning is sought by studying the lives of our forebears, ourselves, and our children and grandchildren. As Nicolas Berdyaev has indicated, "Man is in the highest degree an historical being. He is situated in history and history is situated in him. Between man and history there exists such a deep, mysterious, primordial and coherent relationship, such a concrete inter-dependence, that a divorce between them is impossible. It is as impos-sible to detach man from history and to consider him abstractly as it is to detach history from man and to examine it from without, that is, from a non-human point of view. Nor is it possible to consider man isolated from the profoundest spiritual reality of history."[3] We thus cannot by-pass the challenge of history; we must recognize the mysterious relation-ship between time and eternity.

As historical creatures, we are suspended between our desire for dog-matic certainties and our doubts and despair. We interpret history in the midst of this restless tension. Nevertheless, like Jacob, we continue to wrestle with our destiny, seeking to solve the riddle of our existence. "Actually, the purpose of a historical understanding," says Orthodox historian Georges Florovsky, "is not so much to detect the Divine action in history as to understand the human action, that is, human activities, in the bewildering variety and confusion in which they appear to a human observer. Above all, *the Christian historian will regard history at once as a mystery and as a tragedy—a mystery of salvation and a tragedy of sin.* He will insist on the comprehensiveness of our conception of man, as a pre-requisite of our understanding of his existence, of his exploits, of his destiny, which is actually wrought in his history."[4] Living in the presence of the Eighth Day, our past, present, and future meet and challenge us to realize our potential as children of God created in the Divine image.

Created in the image of God, we view our history not as a spectacle or puppet performance, but as a process in which we are ultimately in-volved. Our involvement historically has revealed both our creativity to accomplish good and our capacity to do evil. Our ability to oscillate between goodness and destruction points not only to our freedom but also to our fallen nature. Both our freedom and fall are not absolute categories but are subject to and related to God's providence. Without acknowledging the presence of the Eighth Day, we are likely to consider our history exclusively from the standpoint of either freedom or the Fall. Either viewpoint per se is false and idolatrous in character. The cult of freedom, as well as the cult of original sin, will not direct us to a viable understanding of our history and destiny.

A further point must be made regarding our fall; H. Butterfield delineates it in *Christianity and History:*

Those who do not believe in the doctrine of the Fall can hardly deny that human history has always been history under the terms and conditions of the Fall. Those who write history as though the world went wrong at the Renaissance, or as though it was the Reformation which spoiled everything, or as though things took the wrong turn at the beginning of the Age of Reason, are suffering from a delusion—history is always a story in which Providence is countered by human aberration. On the other hand, part of the horror which men feel when they look to the possible future is due to a lack of elasticity, an unwillingness to imagine that life can still hold its essential values when our local historical order has been superseded. It is simply a distrust of the resources of Providence.[5]

For the Christian, the Fall must be taken seriously, but it does not preclude either our freedom or God's will to surprise us.

The Fall, according to Professor Gordon Kaufman, should be considered historically, not mythically, "as an event of many generations' duration that happened to the species *homo sapiens* in its historical development; and its consequences are still with us. As the Bible suggests, the fall antedated all civilization, determining its idolatrous character."[6] The date of the Fall is not necessary, but the fact that it did occur in history is important as we appraise God's revelation within the historical process.

Only if the Fall is understood *historically*—and not merely as myth, however profound—will its full significance and meaning be perceived. Moreover, only thus will it become evident why man's salvation also can come—indeed, if there is to be salvation, must come—through further developments in the historical process, through a salvation-history. The Christian faith is eminently historical not only because it sees man's being as radically immersed in history; but because it understands that the evil from which man must be saved is a diseasedness and contamination of this historical process and historical being, which man himself has effected through his historical action; and because it believes in a salvation not *from* history but precisely *of* this history and the man inextricably bound up with it. When understood as the expression of a thoroughly historical perspective, Christian theology is a consistent and profound interpretation of human existence. To regard the Fall as myth rather than in some sense genuine history shatters both the consistency and the meaning of the Christian faith.[7]

Professor Kaufman has rightly emphasized the historic nature of the fall. However, he overstates his case by ruling out any mythical dimension within history.

To stress the historic character of the Fall is to state primarily a theological fact rather than a historic fact. Actually, the Fall is beyond empirical verification; it is instead an attempt to relate to human beings a meaningful story of historic and personal value. This theological intent steers us between dogmatism and despair as we seek to make sense out of our existence.

The presence of the Eighth Day does not enable us to pinpoint empirically "the hand of God" in secular history. This vagueness might be alarming to some, but to claim otherwise is to commit idolatry. Historian Herbert Butterfield indicated that we cannot find the hand of God in secular history unless we have first believed in God in our personal experience.[8] It is not possible to detect a specific type of Divine activity in history unless we already through the "eyes of faith" are committed to the belief that God acts in such ways.[9] History does not convey to us any notion about God beyond the theological biases we bring to our study of history. However,

> if it is objected that God is revealed in history through Christ, I cannot think that this can be true for the mere external observer, who puts on the thinking-cap of the ordinary historical student. It only becomes effective for those who have carried the narrative to intimate regions inside themselves, where certain of the issues are brought home to human beings. In this sense our interpretation of the human drama throughout the ages rests finally on our interpretation of our most private experience of life, and stands as merely an extension to it. At the same time I am not sure that any part of history has been properly appropriated until we have brought it home to ourselves in the same intimate way, so that it has been knit into one fabric continuous with our inner experience.[10]

In short, we are called upon to integrate personal and cosmic history, but not to be dismayed if our particular understanding is not accepted by others in the intellectual marketplace.

All historical accounts are prejudiced interpretations. It cannot be otherwise if the materials are arranged in any coherent pattern. Historical inquiry is a retrospective vision in which one's faith suppositions play an active role. Historical interpretations are literally beyond verification; we can never go back to the event as it really happened. Hence philosophical or theological assumptions, whether secular or biblical in origin, attempt to supply the norms necessary in order to tell a meaningful story of our future in the light of our past.[11] The very nature of historical study motivates the prudent student to carefully balance between dogmatism and despair in seeking to unfold the mystery and meaning of God's revelation in human history.[12]

The Reformation and Orthodoxy

The Protestant Reformation has been interpreted as an attempt to re-assert the dynamism of the Eighth Day in human history. Was God actually making history at the Reformation? Our previous discussion has warned us that empirical verification of God's involvement in human history is impossible to ascertain with dogmatic certainty. In each of our traditions we must constantly discern between "historical certainty" and the "certainty of faith." "These two lie on different levels," Wolfhart Pannenberg explains, "and therefore there is no essential contradiction in basing a sure trust on an event which we can know historically only with probability. Historical research can never achieve definitive certainty in its results, but only greater or less probability. Formally that is true of all possible objects of historical examination, and has nothing to do with the special characteristic of a particular historical theme. But the certainty of faith, on the other hand, depends on the peculiarity of a particular historical event, namely, the history of Jesus."[13] The reformers feared the loss of this saving history of Jesus witnessed in the Eighth Day within the church, and wished to maintain it.

The Orthodox have generally tended to discount the Reformation as largely a squabble within the "Christian West." For the Orthodox the earlier schism between Rome and Constantinople was the greater tragedy. "Seen in the light of what happened in the West throughout the Middle Ages and the Renaissance, the Orthodox historian," according to Father John Meyendorff, cannot avoid "considering the schism between Rome and Constantinople as the fundamental, the basic tragedy in the history of Christianity through which the whole of the Christian West lost its theological and spiritual balance. The Orthodox East was often led to adopt toward the West an attitude of sufficiency, and this is un-doubtedly our—very human—sin; for it belongs to the very essence of Catholicity to share in the brother's problems and to help him in resolving them before rushing into anathemas and condemnations."[14] Contacts during this period between the Reformers and the Orthodox were at a minimum; no sustained exchanges took place.[15]

The lack of any continued dialogue between the Reformers and the Orthodox was unfortunate; together they could have explored the nature of the church's catholicity. Also they could have asked together if there were any common criteria to determine what God is doing in human history. Does God make history? If so, how do we know it? Is history no more than the history of the transmission of traditions? Questions such as these are ecumenical in nature and applicable to all Christians.

In reply to these questions, Luther and Calvin sought to reassert the universality and finality of Jesus Christ within the finitude of human history. The scandal of particularity associated with the incarnation became once again the freeing Word, the good news of God's self-revelation to us. Yet God, for both Luther and Calvin, was the *deus absconditus,* the God who hides in the midst of self-revelation. Therefore, the Eighth Day is also filled with both mystery and meaning. We live in its presence, but we do not comprehend entirely its glory as we are baptized into the new aeon. It is not without significance that the Reformers, Luther and Calvin, insisted on letting "God be God" (*soli deo gloria*).

For Luther the very concealment of God in history pressed for an unveiling of God. The secret of God will cease in the *eschaton.* "The masks behind which God's omnipotent presence is now concealed will fall, yes, they will cease to exist," Peter Brunner wrote about Luther's impact on this century. "The struggle between God and the prince of this world cannot remain undecided. It will finally end because it is already fundamentally decided. What we experience as world history will finally be rolled together like a mantle and be laid aside forever. And God's kingdom and Jesus' victory as the fruit of that which the triune God has created within world history through Word and Sacrament as His new creation will be revealed."[16] For Luther, then, faith must not only be built upon history, but this very history is a holy masquerade with the final unmasking left to God.

Although sharing Luther's outlook and indebted to him, Calvin was able to give a more systematic and political expression to his sense of history. Influenced by his scholastic, legal, and humanistic studies, he formulated his thoughts with precision, but at the same time rejected the reasonable but static view of history conditioned by the scholasticism practiced by the Roman Catholic church of his time. E. Harris Harbison wrote that Calvin's "understanding of history, like his understanding of other great Christian doctrines, was an attempt to expound the biblical answer according to the best scholars' consensus, in terms so clear and convincing that Christians would be moved to action by it."[17] Calvin's sense of history was theocentric from its core, but also specific and concrete in its expression.

For example, Calvin saw the Reformation as a specific expression of God making history as we enter the last or decisive stage toward God's *eschaton.* Calvin took Luther's sense of history and with more exactness transformed it into a sense of destiny, Harbison says. "He took the idea of revival or rebirth, which was not much more than a scholarly theory of cultural revival in humanism, with pietistic overtones in Erasmus, and not much more than a mystical expectation in Joachitism, and transformed it into a powerful ideology which could move multitudes. To Calvin, even more self-consciously than to Luther, the present moment was a decisive moment of time in the realization of God's Kingdom, a *Kairos,* a crisis reached in the fullness of time, like the age of the Prophets or the age of the Apostles. (Calvin often felt a close kinship with the Prophets and with David.) So his conception of history became a strong stimulus to action, here, now in this world."[18] Calvin rescued "history from both chance and determinism, and left it in the predestining power of the living God."[19] He found himself at any given moment before a crossroads, confronted by his eschatological vision and the immediate concerns of his city-state of Geneva.

Contemporary Lutheran and Reformed theologians might well adhere more seriously to the eschatological vision *and* tension that the Reformers experienced. Discussions on the "theology of hope" by Protestant theologians contain both a necessary truth and falsehood in this emphasis. The rediscovery of an eschatological dimension in understanding God's revelation within the historical process is an important corrective to the previous neglect in Western pragmatic "this-worldly" zeal. However, the overemphasis upon eschatology, according to Professor Emeritus George Hendry of Princeton, "threatens to end in a 'pan-eschatological dream'—which is, in fact, a dream. The New Testament is not all written in the future sense; it has a perfect at the heart of it, and this perfect is the key to the future."[20] Orthodoxy for her part has always been an eschatologically oriented church of the Spirit without forfeiting historical perspective. The relationship of a theology of hope to history might prove to be a fruitful avenue of dialogue in the future between Augustinian-centered churches in the West and the patristic traditions of the East, as they together discern God's revelation within the historical process.

Yet the churches of the Reformation can be of service to Orthodoxy as the latter turns a more critical eye to the history of transmission of her own traditions. The problem of history for Orthodoxy, Theodore Stylianopoulos writes, is that "orthodox theology has not yet sufficiently become aware nor has it raised the question of how ancient documents are legitimately examined and how the results of such examination of ancient documents (i.e., their historical meaning) can be evaluated and applied to contemporary life. The larger context of these two basic questions, of which the West is highly aware, is the question of the meaning of history and the value of ancient documents such as the Bible for contemporary life."[21] Unless Orthodoxy critically and constructively views its sources, how reliable and meaningful is it to speak of God's revelation in history?

East-West dialogue cannot progress further without challenging Orthodoxy concerning the patristic categories through which biblical revelation is interpreted. Protestants' extensive experience with historical criticism may be of assistance at this point. Such explorations into historical criticism, and its implications, Stylianopoulos says, will come "into serious conflict not only with traditional Orthodox views concerning the interpretation of the Bible, but also with the concept of the immutability of Christian doctrine. It may be that historical critical studies will ultimately strengthen the position of Orthodoxy, since the latter is fundamentally apophatic with an existential rather than a metaphysical bent. However, this stage will not be reached until after a period of intra-Orthodox debate during which Orthodox scholars must deal with those tensions and conflicts, i.e., with the problem of history for Orthodoxy."[22]

Ultimately, both East and West must give greater attention to the primary sources of revelation. Perhaps the most fundamental question for all traditions is that of revelation itself. Without understanding the nature of revelation fully, are we not in danger of uncritically establishing history as the fundamental category? In our apologetic concerns with secular life, we may be guilty of setting history above revelation in our desire to show that divine revelation has historical support. Revelation transcends history while in history. Revelation consists of the speech of God as well as the acts of God. Does the nature of revelation require that history stand absolutely as the supreme milieu of God's revelation? While there exists the scandal of particularity in the incarnation, perhaps the equally scandalous factor that is sidestepped is the direct verbal communication of revelation as evidenced in the call of Abraham, dreams, prophecy, and visions that are also found in the biblical records. God is revealed in varied forms.

History is not the only category through which we receive and regulate God's revelation. When our dependence on history is overworked at the exclusion of any other axis of interpretation for God's revelation, then we are pressed into what James Barr calls artificial "distinctions between *Geschichte* and *Historie*, between *Heilsgeschichte* and *Weltgeschichte*, or the artificiality of *Sage* and *Augeschichte* as used by Barth of the creation stories. And this artificiality in past discussion seems in prospect to lead to a law of diminishing returns; each new refinement on a conception of history both theologically regulative and also set on a level biblical base seems only to make it more unlikely that a consensus will ever be reached."[23] Will the influence of Wolfhart Pannenberg or Gordon Kaufman in their attempts to write a historicist perspective of theology lead to any greater degree of agreement?

In light of the Eighth Day, Reformed, Roman Catholic, and Orthodox traditions must recognize the dangers of reading their theological affirmations solely through the category of history or imposing their historical "conclusions" upon theology. The nature of the Christian faith is such that neither emphasis should rule over the other. To maintain both axes of interpretation will prove a more reliable guide in understanding both God's revelation and the historical process. The categories of history and revelation are both filled with meaning and mystery. The eschatological dimension of the Eighth Day will warn all traditions from finalizing either their theological or historical findings. Indeed, we must confess, with the apostle Paul, that we perceive the truth myopically and astigmatically.

The Role of the Holy Spirit
in History

The Eighth Day in human history is a testimony of salvation-history witnessed in baptism and the Lord's Supper; this day also announces that we live in the aeon of the Spirit. The Christian symbolism of baptism, according to Willy Rordorf, "underlined the fact that with the resurrection the eighth day had already dawned, that the Holy Spirit in full abundance had already come and that on every eighth day, i.e. on every Sunday, he was truly experienced in the administration of baptism."[24] To live in the presence of the Eighth Day was to live in the presence of the Spirit. From the standpoint of cosmic or universal history, the Spirit was also present at creation as part of the unfolding mystery of the triune God. The Eighth Day is the "first day" from the eschatological perspective of God. We should not limit the advent of the Spirit to the advent of Christ. For that matter, to speak of any "advent" is to refer to time from a human viewpoint. This was the error according to some Orthodox interpretations in the *filioque* clause that the East rejected. From a divine perspective there really is no "advent." While it is true to say that we live in the aeon of the Spirit, remember that the

Spirit has been a part of the historical process from the beginning. With God there is not beginning or end; to speak of time in relation to God is to admit the limitations of human theologizing. The Orthodox distinction between essence and energy in relation to God indicates this human limitation in theologizing as does also its theological methodology—the apophatic or negative approach in contrast to the kataphatic or affirmative theology of the West.

Parenthetically, it might be suggested that this organic link between the Spirit and history was providentially brought to our attention within our "space age" when the astronauts on Apollo 8 (Anders, Borman, and Lovell) read on a Christmas Eve the first ten verses of Genesis: "In the beginning God created the heavens and the earth. The earth was without form and void, and darkness was upon the face of the deep; and the Spirit of God was moving over the face of the waters." Reading these verses on Christmas Eve while gazing at their primordial view of the lunar landscape below was indeed suggestive. Explorers wished to make sense out of their expanding cosmos and look back in faith to their beginnings. The moving Spirit of God at creation is also the same Spirit present at our rebirth in baptism and the Spirit whose *prodding* will lead us to our *eschaton*.

More specifically within the present *ecclesial structures* of our respective traditions, we should remind ourselves of the challenging presence of the Holy Spirit which leads us in history to do God's will. Fulfilling the Divine will is our goal or *eschaton* as churches. Hence in the future, Protestant, Orthodox, and Roman Catholic encounters must discover as never before the organic union between "the Holy Spirit and the Catholicity of the Church."[25] Uppsala rightly pointed out "that catholicity can properly be understood only in connection with pneumatology. The Holy Spirit is the origin and source of true catholicity. It is He who makes the Church a really authoritative witness in this world; thus any consideration of catholicity must be accompanied by the question of 'what the Spirit is saying to the churches' today."[26] There is no doubt that the Holy Spirit witnesses to the saints of all generations, uniting them for the sake of the church's catholicity. It should not surprise anyone to hear the claim that the communion of saints already enjoys catholicity, a qualitative state of ecumenicity beyond our present imagination.

Official dialogues with the Orthodox by Anglicans, Lutherans, Reformed, and Catholics must be constantly aware of this organic union between the Holy Spirit and the catholicity of the church. Ignoring this would lead to despair; awareness will be a source of support in discouraging moments of doctrinal disparity. The presence of the Holy Spirit reminds all dialogists that renewal and authentic catholicity are approached through mutual repentance. Catholicity in its fullness is a gift of the Holy Spirit; it cannot be grasped by any individual or any single church. The Holy Spirit, as the universal bishop of the church, ensures unity in diversity. A second Pentecost, like the first, will be essentially a divine rather than a human event. Such realization should humble us in present discourses and fortify us in continuing our pilgrimage.

Past encounters indicate the need for more study and effort to develop a common language of discourse in a shrinking world; equally important is greater determination to escape entrenched defenses. We must learn to trust one another in our common pursuit of the truth. Today's encounters oscillate between suspicion and sincerity. Overcoming suspicion will enable our future dialogues to proceed more rapidly toward the promised Pentecost of renewal.

Orthodoxy's ecumenical dilemma is whether to retreat to the womb of the Mother Church or advance amiably with non-Orthodox to the point, some fear, of apostasy. According to Orthodox theologian William Schneirla, "Both speak from positions of anxiety and lack of faith, and one need not look far in our history to find abundant reasons for negativism if not despair. The challenge of ecumenism is more disarming than the temptations of the past: either Paul VI or Eugene Blake is more appealing than Abdul Hamid or Joseph Stalin, and the call of Christian unity is an answer to Orthodox prayer."[27] Orthodox and non-Orthodox alike must avoid substituting sentimentality for love or pragmatic considerations for truth, as they seek to deepen their desire for unity. The day of polite evasions on both sides has passed. In short, a renewed look at the past will support the familiar but neglected truth that the past, present, and future are related parts to the whole of life and grace as witnessed by the Holy Spirit who moves within history fulfilling the will of the Lord of the Eighth Day.

Discerning the will of the Lord in human history is a difficult task at best. Our next chapter dramatizes this difficulty as illustrated in the case of Patriarch Cyril Lucaris's Calvinistic Confession.

3

Patriarch Lucaris's Calvinistic Confession

Patriarch Cyril Lucaris's case history not only serves as a significant confessional encounter between Orthodox and Reformed traditions but also illustrates the inherent dangers when theological boundaries are crossed. Previous research on Lucaris has been both polemical and anti-ecumenical.[1] Today, there is a need for an ecumenical understanding of this vital figure and his seventeenth-century *Confession of Faith* to serve as a fruitful platform for Christians of Eastern and Western traditions in this age of convergence.

The theological merit of the *Confession* was subordinated to the obvious political instrument it had become during the seventeenth century in the hands of Protestants with their battle against Roman Catholics. There is no doubt that Lucaris was influenced by Protestant diplomats and theologians at Constantinople and Alexandria. Admittedly, he was seeking Christian unity and rapprochement, but he was also motivated by political considerations, caught as he was between the theological and political cross fire of Protestants and Roman Catholics under a non-Christian, Turkish rulership.

Lucaris's *Confession* was later condemned by a series of councils during the half century following his death, and it thus provoked Orthodoxy's first historic confessional reaction to the Reformation. It also prompted the Orthodox to examine the content of their theological thoughts; this had not been done seriously since their previous major confrontation with the West at the Council of Ferrara-Florence (1438–39) prior to the Reformation. Patriarch Cyril Lucaris's controversial *Confession* within our present environment might indeed have stimulating and useful implications for future East-West dialogue. Our discussion will proceed along the following outline: first, a closer look at Lucaris and his times;

second, a commentary and critique of his *Confession;* and third, the implications of confessions for our day.

The Man and His Times

Constantine Lucaris was born on the island of Crete in the town of Candia on November 13, 1572. He was a younger contemporary of another famous Cretan, El Greco, the painter. He gave up his baptismal name of "Constantine" and took up the name of "Cyril" at the time of his ordination into the priesthood in 1595. His father, a prosperous butcher, was determined to give his son the best education available. For Cretans, under Venetian rule, this meant going to Venice to attend the Greek school at the age of twelve. He received excellent training in Latin and Greek and was later enrolled as a student at the University of Padua, the center of Neo-Aristotelianism. He passed his examinations with honor and decided upon the priesthood, since he had little taste for commerce or medicine, the more popular careers among educated young Greeks of his time. His decision to follow a priestly career was confirmed by an encouraging letter from his cousin Meletius Pegas, elected in 1590 to the patriarchal throne of Alexandria.[2]

Following his ordination, church authorities at Constantinople, concerned over the fate of the Orthodox in Poland, sent Cyril and a companion (Nicephorus Cantacuzenus) as exarchs to support the Orthodox faithful. However, the mission was largely unsuccessful, since nearly all the Orthodox bishops there had already submitted to the demand of the Polish Catholic king that they accept the primacy of the pope in the famous Brest-Litovsk Union of 1596; this in a substantial way signaled the effective advent of Eastern rite churches (called Uniate churches). Cyril and his companion decided in any case to stay on in Poland and to give whatever assistance they could to the Orthodox faithful. The king's agents, however, held them under careful watch and a short time afterward denounced them as Turkish spies. Cyril escaped; his companion was arrested and put to death. This brief sojourn in Poland introduced Cyril to the toughness of Roman Catholic policy and also provided his first contact with Protestants—a discussion with Lutherans on the question of Christian unity. He also approached the question of Christian unity with the Catholics; this latter correspondence was used against him by the Jesuit Peter Scarga some seventeen years later to undermine his position among his fellow Orthodox.

Leaving Poland, Cyril was invited to Egypt, where in 1601 he was elected to succeed Meletius Pegas to the Alexandrian Patriarchate before his thirtieth birthday. Cyril, an efficient patriarch, reigned for nearly two decades, moving the seat of the patriarchate from Alexandria to Cairo, the governmental center of the province. While in Egypt, he began what later became a stimulating friendship with several Dutchmen led by Cornelius van Haag, who later became the ambassador at the Dutch Embassy in Constantinople. Van Haag introduced Cyril to Jan Uytenbogaert, a Dutch theologian and a pupil of Arminius. The correspondence that resulted pointed to a growing sympathy for Protestant doctrine.

From Egypt, Cyril made frequent trips to Constantinople. During these years the Constantinopolitan Patriarchate was occupied by Neophytus II and Raphel II, both of whom favored union with Rome. Steven Runciman writes, "When Neophytus licensed an Italian Greek's sermon which openly advocated union, Cyril was asked to preach the counter-blast and to remain in Constantinople to direct anti-Roman activities. He was there when Neophytus died in January 1612. A majority in the Synod elected him to succeed to the Patriarchate. But he could not or would not pay the sum demanded by the Sublime Porte for the confirmation of his election. His opponents on the Synod therefore put up a rival candidate, Timothy, Bishop of Marmora, who promised the Sultan and his ministers a sum of larger than was usual; and the synod was ordered to elect him."[3] Cyril retired to Mount Athos for a short time, visited Wallachia, and then returned to Egypt, where he now began correspondence with Calvinistic Archbishop of Canterbury George Abbot, who invited him to send a few young Greeks to England to study theology. In response, Cyril sent a Macedonian young man named Metrophanes Kritopoulos to England.

In the meantime, Patriarch Timothy from Constantinople continued to feel threatened by Cyril. Patriarch Timothy attempted to stir up trouble for Cyril by denouncing him as a Lutheran. "Cyril answered that, as Timothy knew nothing of Luther nor of his doctrine, he had no idea how far it might resemble his own; he had better keep quiet."[4] Cyril visited Constantinople again in 1620, probably following a reconciliation with Timothy. While Cyril was there, Timothy suddenly died, shortly after attending a dinner party given by Cyril's friend the Dutch Ambassador, Cornelius van Haag. "The Jesuits promptly circulated a rumor that van Haag had poisoned him in order to leave the throne vacant for Cyril," Runciman says. "If this were so, the Holy Synod certainly did not object. Cyril was promptly and unanimously elected Patriarch. On this occasion he paid the required sum to the Sublime Porte."[5] Thus began Cyril's stormy and creative period on and off the Patriarchal See in Constantinople until his final imprisonment and execution in June of 1638.

During this period, Cyril had powerful friends in the Dutch and English ambassadors. Cyril was later to show his deep appreciation to Sir Thomas Roe, the English ambassador, by asking him to present as a gift to King Charles I of England the famous manuscript of the Bible known as the *Codex Alexandrinus,* which Cyril had originally brought with him from Alexandria.

Cyril also had powerful enemies during this time, namely the Jesuits, who had the support of the French ambassador, the Comte de Cesi. Interpreters of Lucaris such as Archbishop Germanos, who was Metropolitan (head of church) of Thyateira, put forth the thesis that Cyril was a victimized patriarch caught in the Orthodox East.[6] Germanos's conclusion was that Cyril's "long and versatile activity presents numerous contradictions and lapses, due to the opportunism of his political tactics as well as to faults of character. Perhaps he may have failed to reconcile his duty as the Primate of the Orthodox Church with the exigencies of high politics and with his aims as spiritual leader of his Nation. Yet no one can deny that Lucaris, so sorely tried by Fortune, succeeded, by his long and patriotic exertions, in educating and receiving the national consciousness of the Greek people and in pointing the way toward new horizons in the life of the Nation."[7] In short, Germanos saw Cyril as a national folk hero who, along with his faults, was largely a prisoner of his time. This conclusion merits consideration, but underplays the theological contribution made by Lucaris as a theologian and churchman.

During Cyril's reign as patriarch, his concern to improve education was high on his list of priorities. He reformed the Patriarchal Academy, which meant that Greek boys were less dependent upon Jesuit establishments for quality education. He sought and obtained a printing press. Once obtained, the press began to publish theological works in Greek, mostly anti-Roman tracts. The Catholics were naturally not pleased with this, since Pope Urban VIII had established a Greek press under the direction of the Jesuits and the *Congregatio de Propaganda Fide.* Roman forces actively worked to oust Cyril. This reached its climax under the efforts of Holy Roman Ambassador Rudolph Schmid-Schwarzenhorn, who plotted Cyril's execution by bribing the grand vizier, Bairam Pasha, who accused Lucaris of treason before the sultan.

Before the final curtain fell on Cyril's career, he was able to publish the first modern Greek translation of the New Testament. The new translation was regarded as dangerous by many of his churchmen, who considered scripture to be reserved for biblical experts. His bishops became most alarmed following the publication of his *Confession of Faith,* first in a Latin translation at Geneva in March 1629 and dedicated to van Haag. Later this was followed by a Greek text written in Cyril's own hand and dated 1631. This copy is preserved at the University of Geneva Library.[8] Translations into other languages soon followed. Not since the *De Fide Orthodoxa* of John of Damascus had such a piece of work been produced by an Orthodox. Many within Lucaris's church, however, saw no need for adding to the statements of John of Damascus and the decrees of the early ecumenical councils. Thus, Lucaris had not only foreign powers to contend with but also mounting pressure opposing him within his own household.

Confronted by this situation of growing unrest, Catholics began to press what they clearly saw to be their advantage by making known widely the contents of the *Confession* within the environs of Constantinople. According to Runciman, "Within a few months there was a conspiracy against the Patriarch planned by no less than five of his metropolitans. It resulted in the elevation to the Patriarchate in October 1633 of Cyril Contari, Metropolitan of Berrhoea (Aleppo). However, Cyril Contari had promised 50,000 dollars to the Sublime Porte to secure his election, and he could not raise the money. After a few days he gave up the effort and was exiled to Tenedos. From there he wrote an apology to Cyril Lucaris, who restored him to his see."[9] The attacks upon Lucaris were not ended, as Cyril Contari tried again and for a time succeeded as Patriarch Cyril II, while Lucaris was exiled for fifteen months on Rhodes.

Lucaris, however, was not without friends, especially the Dutch ambassador. In March, 1636, Cyril II held a council at Constantinople which anathematized Cyril I as a heretic; however, the Holy Synod was soon suspicious of Cyril II's relations with Rome. In June 1636 it met to depose him; he was exiled to Rhodes and his ship returned with Lucaris. Meanwhile Neophytus, Metropolitan of Heraclea, was elected patriarch. A loyal friend of Cyril I, he took on the office temporarily in order to arrange for the cancellation of the anathema. In March, 1637, Cyril Lucaris was again patriarch.[10]

In retrospect, this was only a momentary victory for Lucaris. During the fifteen months in Rhodes he had lost influence, and his views had aroused polemic attitudes among the Greeks. In addition, his foreign friends Sir Thomas Roe, Ambassador van Haag, and Antoine Leger had left Constantinople. Lucaris's position was in reality greatly weakened. At this point Ambassador Schmid-Schwarzenhorn and the Jesuits were able to influence key Greeks and Turks to their cause for the final ouster of Lucaris.

On June 20, 1638, on orders from Sultan Murad IV, Cyril Lucaris was arrested, and five days later he was strangled by the Sultan's Janissary Guards on a small boat in the Bosphorus. The next day, according to the custom of the guards, Lucaris's possessions were sold in the marketplace and thus his fate became known to the people. "Angry crowds of Greeks massed outside of Cyril Contari's door, crying 'Pilate, give us the body,'" Runciman says. "To prevent a riot the Governor told the soldiers to exhume the body. They did so, but flung it into the sea. There some Greek fishermen found it and recovered it. It was buried in the little monastery of Saint Andrew on an island off the Asiatic coast."[11]

The Sultan appointed Lucaris's old adversary, Cyril Contari, as patriarch again. He promptly held a council in which Cyril Lucaris's views were again anathematized. A few months later Cyril II signed a paper giving his allegiance to Pope Urban VII. When news of this leaked out, both the Holy Synod of bishops and the Sultan were furious. Cyril II was shortly thereafter deposed, branded a heretic, and exiled to North Africa, where he died. The condemnation against Lucaris's *Confession*, however, did not cease as it was placed under further disrepute in subsequent councils at Constantinople, Jassy, and Jerusalem. In fact, in Jerusalem, Patriarch Dositheos condemned the *Confession* but expressed some doubts as to whether Lucaris was indeed its author. At Jerusalem, it was even said in his behalf that there were ten thousand witnesses of his well-known piety. Thus the name of Cyril Lucaris has caused both frustration and praise in the minds of Orthodox believers.

Lucaris's Confession— Commentary and Critique

In writing his *Confession* (see Appendix), Cyril Lucaris was not setting precedent; as already mentioned, there was the *De Fide Orthodoxa* of John of Damascus. Also, Patriarch Gennadius prepared a statement of Orthodox beliefs after the fall of Constantinople, at the request of Sultan Mehmet the Conqueror; Patriarch Jeremias II presented a response to the Lutherans; and Metrophones Kritopoulos prepared his *Confession of Faith*. Statements of faith stemming from the patriarchal office commanded respect and prestige within the Orthodox tradition, but they were not regarded as binding on the church unless endorsed by an ecumenical council. Hence the statements of belief or confessions were seen as authoritative opinions from informed sources.

From this perspective, Lucaris's *Confession* of eighteen articles was designed to serve as a guide, not to enunciate dogma. His aim was to strengthen those in the Orthodox church against Romanizing tendencies and to lay the groundwork for a reforming church. Lucaris was trying to accomplish this reform single-handedly, without the aid of a council or Holy Synod. Finally, related to his reforming desire, he wished to have a document that would provide a basis for negotiations with non-Orthodox churches.

The high points of the *Confession* are the following. (1) It affirms the Trinity without the *filioque* clause. This is in keeping with Orthodoxy's long-standing objection to the *filioque* in its understanding of pneumatology. (2) He placed the authority of scripture over the authority of the church. This is contrary to the conciliar understanding of authority in Orthodoxy; however, the emphasis upon the Holy Spirit as the final guide is in keeping with Orthodoxy. (3) Cyril accepted the doctrine of predestination and election; this position, within Orthodoxy's apophatic method of theologizing, no doubt would be objectionable. (4) God is the creator of everything, but God is not the author of evil. Orthodox would find this generally acceptable, but an apophatic outlook would be uncomfortable with such an explicit statement.

(5) God's providence is beyond our comprehension and analysis. Orthodoxy would agree that this is in keeping with the apophatic mentality. (6) Original sin is universal. Orthodoxy would agree in its understanding of the Fall. (7) Jesus Christ is God and man, the redeemer and the judge to come. This view is in agreement with the Nicene-Constantinopolitan Creed. (8) Jesus Christ is the sole mediator, high priest, and head of the church. Orthodoxy would essentially agree. (9) Justification by faith in Christ is necessary for salvation. This statement differs from the Orthodox understanding of *theosis*, which presents justification as a continuing gift of the Spirit. (10) The head of the church is Christ; he rules over the faithful both living and dead. (11) Lucaris also pointed out that among the faithful there are hypocrites who are not among the elect. This article touches upon the question of the visible and invisible church. While Orthodoxy may assent in principle to the concerns mentioned, the explicitness violates the mystical visibility of the church stressed in the East.

(12) The church can err, but it is spared by constant submission to the Holy Spirit, the inspirer of the church and the indwelling Spirit of Christ, who judges the external and internal visibility of the church. However, confession of error might seem threatening to Orthodoxy's claim that it is the undivided, unbroken tradition of the one church created at Pentecost. (13) While we are justified by faith, works are not to be ignored, since they testify to faith. Orthodoxy would agree that both faith and works are needed. (14) Free will in the unregenerate is dead, and they are incapable of doing good; the regenerate do good with the assistance of grace. Today, most Christians, including the Orthodox, would not be so quick to place exact limits upon God's grace in operation. (15) Only two sacraments were instituted by Christ and recorded in the New Testament. These sacraments are baptism and the Eucharist, which alone are the efficacious means of grace through faith. It is true to say that baptism (always accompanied by confirmation in the Orthodox tradition) and the Eucharist are generally considered the essential sacraments in Orthodoxy. Only after the thirteenth century did the other sacraments receive recognition by the Orthodox, but those were given a subordinate position to baptism and the Eucharist. The number of sacraments is actually an open-ended question in Orthodoxy.

(16) Baptism is necessary for the remission of both original and actual sin. Orthodox would agree. (17) Cyril believed in the real presence of Christ in the Eucharist operating through faith. He denied belief in transubstantiation, since what is apprehended through faith is spiritual, not physical. Orthodoxy looks upon the Eucharist mystically and resents the explicitness doctrinally attached to its practice by Protestants and Catholics. For the Orthodox, Cyril has seemingly fallen into the error of being too explicit. (18) There are only two conditions after death—heaven and hell—and everyone is judged at death. After death there is no second chance. Purgatory is a mere illusion. Those justified by faith suffer no more and those unjustified pass straight to everlasting punishment. While Orthodoxy would not generally disagree with Cyril's position regarding the prospects after death, again from an apopathic stance their tradition would indicate a more reverent agnosticism regarding what plans God had for the souls of the dead, since there is no clear revelation on the final outcome.

In addition to the eighteen articles, an appendix was later attached to clear up Lucaris's stand on the following points: (1) scripture should be available to everyone and read by all; (2) the scriptures are clear to those who have been justified by faith; (3) the canonical books are those listed at the Council of Laodicea; and (4) the cult of images (icons) is condemned since they have been so often misused. Icons are permissible as aids to worship, not as objects of worship.

To sum up, then, the *Confession* and its appendix, it contains no doctrine specifically denied by any of the ecumenical councils. Nevertheless, the statement of his beliefs definitely seems alien to the apophatic tendency of Orthodoxy with its emphasis upon a mystical, reverent agnosticism as opposed to the kataphatic leanings of Western theologizing characteristic in Augustinian thought. In fact, Lucaris's *Confession* can be said to be more Augustinian than Calvinistic, which certainly does not endear his *Confession* to Orthodoxy.[12] Furthermore, it was Lucaris's intention to protect his church from Rome; instead, many were shocked to see Orthodox faith so explicitly and unambiguously stated. This was contrary to the Orthodox spirit and the Byzantine style of being less rationalistic for the sake of economy and *symphonia* (harmony).

The Orthodox could accept without much debate the following articles: (1) on the procession of the Holy Spirit; (4) on the creation; (5) on the inscrutability of God's providence; (6) on original sin; (7) and (8) on Christ as the head of the church and redeemer; (10) on the nature of the church; (12) that the church might err without the help of the Holy Spirit; and (16) on the necessity for baptism. Also, most Orthodox would find acceptable the reading of scripture by the *laos* and the list of the canonical books in the appendix.

As to the remainder, Lucaris would find a theological argument on his hands, since Orthodox theologians are themselves not in agreement on these matters. Specifically, I am referring to the number of sacraments in Orthodoxy, the question of transubstantiation, the denial of purgatory in an absolute sense, and the elevation of scriptural authority beyond the authority of councils. Ecumenical councils are necessary to an Orthodox understanding of authority, even though Christians, East and West, may be divided on which councils are ecumenical.

In today's climate of growing cooperation and understanding, Lucaris's omission of the place of unwritten tradition prior to scripture would certainly be questioned. The church as the guardian of tradition is historically prior to a recognized canon of scripture. Lucaris apparently denied this sequence in his *Confession,* which clearly revealed the extent to which Protestant influences acted upon him in the face of his fears of Roman control.

Another reason for the caution shown in accepting Lucaris's

Confession was linked to his views on predestination and election. Runciman explains the two views on these doctrines generally held in Orthodoxy:

> Mark Eugenicus had maintained that God's prescience was absolute but predestination relative; only good actions are predetermined as well as foreknown by God because only they conform to his will. In general the church preferred the rival, more deterministic doctrine of George Scholarius Gennadius: which is, with slightly different terminology, the doctrine of John of Damascus. This holds that prescience precedes predestination. The initiative for good or evil comes from the created will. Predestination is controlled by but does not control God's knowledge and wisdom. This was the view briefly summarized by Jeremias II in his answer to the Lutherans.[13]

Finally, Cyril Lucaris's stress upon justification by faith was really foreign to the Orthodox understanding of what it means to become a Christian. Had Lucaris substituted the word *theosis*, with its broader implications of faith and work integrally related in the believer's pilgrimage, as an interpretation of what it means to be a Christian, he would have found a more receptive audience for his reforming program. Here again, as in the matter of unwritten tradition, Lucaris was not sufficiently creative with the interpretations received from the Protestants. Given the climate of today, Lucaris no doubt would approach his theological concerns differently. As a man of the seventeenth century, his theological resourcefulness and flexibility were remarkable, especially when contrasted to his fellow Orthodox, but even more when measured by the best minds found among Catholic and Protestant leaders of his day.

Cyril Lucaris saw himself as a reforming patriarch, but he was perceived by his contemporaries as a revolutionary. His reforming program did not enjoy today's supportive context of ecumenism. Even with today's spirit, his contemporary successors Ecumenical Patriarchs Athenagoras I and Demetrios I continue to find elements of intransigence among their own people in matters of Christian unity. In every age, Orthodoxy constantly battles with itself in maintaining dialogue without losing identity. Accomplishing this raises one of the basic theological concerns among churches living in our present technologically overexposed world. The case study of Cyril Lucaris also raises for each tradition, East and West, the important question as to the future implications of confession-making for our day.

Are Confessions of Faith
Obsolete?

The *first* implication from Lucaris's case is the obvious vulnerability of Orthodoxy when pressed to explain her *raison d'être*. Lucaris's *Confession* revealed too much Protestant influence, but the subsequent confessions of faith by Peter of Moghila, Metropolitan of Kiev, and Dositheos, Patriarch of Jerusalem, represented a Latinizing tendency.[14] Neither Lucaris's *Confession* nor the confessions that followed were expressive of the indigenous nature of Orthodoxy. The Lucaris episode impressed upon Orthodoxy the need to express her soul, rather than prostitute herself to each passing suitor whose charisma or need dominated the moment. Since Orthodoxy has been for centuries the church in captivity, its basic style of life has been oriented toward survival. This situation in part continues within today's Marxist and Islamic environments. This price, however, may be too high if renewal is truly desired. Confession making requires an authentic expression of one's true identity. What lasting value is there in a church that has lost its ring of authenticity? The church will always be in some form of captivity—religious, ideological, cultural, or technological. The complex context of each age calls the church to know herself and to continue that unbroken tradition of witness within the thought expressions of each age.

As Reformed theologian George Hendry has stated, "The confessional church is the church which recognizes a distinction between the word which it speaks and the word which is spoken to it. The Reformation may be said to have begun with Luther's discovery that the word *to* the church is not identical (in the sense of indistinguishable or interchangeable) with the word *of* the church; it is and remains the word of God, which retains its sovereign freedom to come to the church with saving and renewing power; it is a word to which the church must always listen."[15] Hendry's point is that this distinction is not to be understood as a disjunction. "The word to the church must also become the word of the church; for it is the word which the church is commissioned to speak. It is to this end that the ministry has been divinely instituted in the church, as the *Augsburg Confession* states (Art. V); for the ministry is the instrument of God through which 'he gives the Holy Spirit, who works faith, when and where he pleases, in those who hear the gospel.'"[16] Thus, the role of the confession is to help the church to understand its responsibility in faith before God.

Orthodox theologian Stanley Harakas concurs that the intention of a confession is to aid the church as it seeks to fulfill its mission amidst true and false witnesses. Faithful to the apophatic approach to theologizing, Harakas states that the confession "can better tell what is false than define the essence of the truth. Its creeds and confessions serve better to define what is not rather than what is. The absence of a complete and absolute creed is an inevitable corollary of the fact that Orthodox theology is a negative, apophatic theology. So long as there is paradox, mystery, and the mystical vision of God, creeds and confessions will never be adequate to express the Faith 'once given to the Saints.'"[17] Confession making is therefore a necessary function for all churches as responsive communities before God. At the same time, Orthodoxy's apophatic conditioning will often lead to a less clearly defined confession, which in times of pressure may cause Orthodoxy to repeat the errors of other churches in its struggle to survive.

The *second* implication to be drawn from Lucaris is that confession making is not only a matter of content but also of context. The text of a confession must be effectively integrated to the context of its day. Lucaris endeavored to write a text in the light of the context of his day. His limitations in understanding his day resulted in a rather rigid use of Calvinism which his constituents could not accept. Perhaps he knowingly took this risk in hopes of reforming the church of his day.

He once described the state of his church in a letter, saying, "I am the enemy of ignorance; and although I do not object to a simple and unlearned laity, because I know that men may be saved, although their minds are uncultivated and simple, whilst they fight almost daily against the enemies of the faith, carrying on the conflict, not with arms, but with patience, so as to prove themselves on all points faithful soldiers of Christ; yet it is a great dissatisfaction to me that our pastors and bishops should be sunk in the darkness of ignorance."[18] Cyril Lucaris was certainly mindful of his environment, but he was overoptimistic, perhaps even somewhat naive, to hope for any measurable acceptance for his *Confession.* Apart from this calculated risk, the politics of the day were another factor (as always) in the confession-making process.

Turning to our day, we, too, must become increasingly more sensitive to shifting climates as we carry on the responsibilities of confession making today. The knowledge explosion and technological advances contribute daily to the complexity of our situation. Borders and fences are coming down, revealing a wealth of cultural diversity and a pluralism of life-styles upon the earth. Adequate awareness of this expanding and simultaneously shrinking planet is necessary in our search for confessional identity as Christians.

Existentially, this was an experience that Presbyterians discovered in their much publicized *Confession of 1967,* which created a degree of polarization within the denomination. Future ecumenical confessions will address even more complex environments as the church seeks to be a meaningful witness to the gospel. Political and ecclesiastical designations are becoming obsolete in a technologically shrinking world. Confession making must take on a global perspective; we must become emotionally and intellectually more accustomed to theologizing for a "global village." Ecclesiastical parochialism will have less meaning for global-minded citizens. Each of us brings a theological hope chest filled with the traditions and treasures of yesterday. Confession making must relate creatively to the mentality of this hope chest as well as to new consciousness. New consciousness brought about by needs and developments of our shrinking world has created a new type of village Christianity in which we can neither ignore nor accept one another without admitting our theological parochialism.

The *third* implication to be drawn from Lucaris is that each of us must individually examine our own credo. That is to say, we are responsible for working through the confessions and creeds of our heritage and for making our own exegesis of where we stand and why. Essential as ecclesiastical identity is, personal identity is perhaps even more necessary. Each of us is called to write, not in isolation, but through reflection, prayer, and in conversation with our traditions, a synoptic version of the "Gospel According to Myself," as in the tradition of Matthew, Mark, and Luke. Lucaris's *Confession* had its shortcomings; but his writing of this credo for his parishioners is an exercise in responsible discipleship. It is his "Gospel According to Lucaris," which should challenge us. Our calling is to be more than repetitious, copybook Christians who confess yesterday's faith without thinking carefully; such a church will be unrelated to the struggles of life around us.

One's credo in this new day of village Christianity must express both ignorance and hope in a psychologically undogmatic, open-ended, and joyful style, fully aware that God is the final judge in the *eschaton.* From this eschatological perspective all confessions will one day be judged. Our pilgrimage of faith is a matter of risk. "Now we see only puzzling reflections in a mirror, but then we shall see face to face" (1 Cor. 13:12, NEB). From this Pauline perspective, can any of us afford to be other than open-ended Christians toward our future responsibilities in confession making? To be otherwise is to render the entire process of confession making obsolete.

For the present, we can take up the challenge of Lucaris, knowing that "every man worthy of being called a son of man bears his cross and mounts his Golgatha," as Nikos Kazantzakis puts it. "Many, indeed most, reach the first or second step, collapse pantingly in the middle of the Journey, and do not attain the summit—in other words, the summit of their duty: to be crucified, resurrected, and to save their souls. Afraid of crucifixion, they grow fainthearted; they do not know that the cross is the only path to resurrection. There is no other path."[19] It is within this ecumenical framework of pilgrimage that we must view this vital figure and his seventeenth-century *Confession of Faith.*

Patriarch Lucaris was not the first or the last victim among Eastern Christians who suffered for his faith. The history of Eastern Christianity is saturated with suffering and bloodshed at the hands of unfriendly forces alien to Eastern Christian spirituality. The outcome has been a carefully guarded spirituality and tradition in the East, using various means for survival. Closely linked to this discussion of Orthodox confession making is the underlying issue of authority in all Christian traditions, to be discussed in the following chapter.

PART TWO

CHALLENGES TO EASTERN ORTHODOXY AND THE FUTURE

4

The Question of Authority: An Ecumenical Crossroad

We are entering a postinstitutional period. Religious and spiritual fervor outside of institutional structures is increasing. Status quo structures are experiencing acute change. All ecclesiological structures are subject to reexamination. We are at the beginning of a traumatic metamorphosis, with emerging patterns still offstage preparing to make their debut. As a consequence, traditional lines of authority for Protestants, Catholics, and Orthodox are under question and attack.

Authority in Ecumenical Perspective

For Protestants such questioning is not new; authority of the Bible came under massive assault in the nineteenth century through the effort of critical biblical scholarship. Today, Roman Catholic reappraisal of the magisterium is initiating intense debate. Orthodoxy, with its history of harassment, is just beginning to emerge from a defensive to a critical stance regarding its sources of authority.

Authority has always been under question in Christian history.[1] Authority is the unresolved ecumenical issue of the past as well as the present. Perhaps more than any other single factor, it has been responsible for the fragmentation of the *Corpus Christianum* as evidenced, for example, by the splintering nature of the ecumenical councils. Protestants as well as Orthodox study the problem of authority through the context of historical tensions and schisms. Catholics are also beginning to appropriate this viewpoint.

Each tradition in the past took as its authoritative norm certain guidelines that lose their mystery in our present demythologized atmosphere.

The traditional lines of authority for the Orthodox were the ecumenical councils, the early church fathers, and the wholeness of the church; for Roman Catholics, the papacy and its magisterium served as the guardian over the heritage of faith; and for Protestants, authority was largely seen through the biblical confessions and creeds begun in the sixteenth century and continued to the present. Each tradition has stressed the positive values of universality, antiquity, and consensus. Such values are in accord with the famous formula concerning authority by Vincent of Lerins in his *Commonitorium* (chapter 2), *"Quod semper, quod ubique et quod ab omnibus creditum est"* ("That which has been believed always, everywhere, and by everybody"). This formula, however, has not been entirely satisfactory, as evidenced in the ecumenical history of Christians. Let us consider now the unresolved tensions of the present, with particular attention to the Protestant position and some boundary lines of reality for the future.

The Interrelationship of Authority and Hermeneutics

Certainly, authority has functioned as a Christian hermeneutic. The forms of authority are many—the exegete, council, tradition, theologian, pope, and so on. Each in its way seeks to interpret the Christian heritage of revelation in an authoritative manner. Here two basic problems arise: the source of our authority and the transmission of authority. There is constant interaction between authority and hermeneutics; each generation seeks its own interpretation of the gospel and wishes to validate this interpretation by an acceptable authority. The difficulty of agreement on a single authority is the source of anxiety and dilemma for Christians.

Ultimately, the quest for an authoritative interpretation of the gospel is a quest for God. ("For there is no authority except from God . . ." [Rom. 13:1].) Such a pursuit with its search for an omega point of final certitude is not possible for finite humans. Other than God, there is no ultimate authority; pursuit without this recognition can end only in futile disappointment. To fill this vacuum, various ecclesiologies have emerged in the past promising authoritative interpretations for the hesitant pilgrim. Today these comforting structures are under reexamination in our ecumenical era, and theologians are striving to develop a more adequate expression of our faith. Herein, the theologian's hermeneutical contribution is but another human attempt to assert dogmatism over earlier dogmas. In the end, the Christian still lacks a strong authoritative interpretation of faith. In short, it seems that "authorities" are in search of *The Authority*.

Proximate Authority and Protestant Frustration

Protestants have generally dismissed absolute authority as beyond human attainment. They have accommodated themselves to proximate authority and frustration. The frustrations stem largely from the transmission of biblical interpretations. Is there any authoritative norm? The current dialogue between the "new hermeneutic" and its critics is an apt illustration of this transmission problem.[2] Most theologians have left the battle to biblical exegetes, whereas the constructive efforts of both are needed. In any case, Protestants continue to work and live among proximate authorities that are never regarded as final.

To confess that Protestants have no fixed attitudes toward "authoritative interpretations" does not mean that Protestants are subjective anarchists or lack respect for authority. On the contrary, *The Authority* for the Protestant lodges in the revelation of God in Jesus Christ. This revelation has been communicated to us by scripture through the living tradition of the church, past and present. Scripture is not synonymous with revelation; scripture is an interpretation of the revelatory events. The hermeneutician's task is to seek an explanation of the interpretation of revelation. It is precisely here that the hermeneutical task is confronted with the problem of authority. The task of explaining an interpretation of revelation brings us in direct confrontation with the issue of continuity. Who has faithfully conveyed the essence of the revelation through the ages? The answer is the living tradition of the church. Who speaks faithfully for this living tradition? This second question is not so easily answered. Is it the biblical exegete who is keenly conscious that the Bible is the book of the church? Is it the theologian who successfully traces roots of faith back to the apostolic witness? Is it the magisterium, the bishops in their long line of succession? Is it the conscience and consenting will of the *laos,* the people of God? In contemplating these questions we realize the complex interaction and interdependence between scripture and tradition under the sacred canopy of the church.

The ecumenically sophisticated Protestant knows that simply to point to the Bible as the authoritative source does not in fact make it so. Nevertheless, the Protestant continues to stand symbolically with Martin

Luther and the prophets in rejecting any "heteronomous" authority of ecclesiastical structures or courts that demand unswerving obedience to interpretation.[3] This is said in spite of the fact that Protestants, too, have committed questionable deeds in the name of heteronomous authorities; they continue nevertheless to stand with Luther in rejecting imposed authority from any ecclesiastical structure in this ecumenical era.[4]

The Protestant also affirms that anarchy and the self-establishment of "autonomous" authority are equally undesirable. Many Catholics and Orthodox view Luther and his generation as guilty of subjective, autonomous authority. When the Reformers opposed the magisterium and its venerable history of continuity, they indeed did open themselves to vulnerability in this area. In today's climate of reawakening, Protestants are beginning to rediscover their pre-Reformation roots dating from the oral traditions of the church's beginning, expounded in the patristic period and even during the medieval age. The spirit of Protestant catholicity cannot and should not be limited to the event of the Reformation in the sixteenth century. The authority of Luther, Calvin, and others is of no avail except to the extent that they faithfully continue the noble tradition of the early church fathers who also attempted to transmit faithfully the apostolic witness. The reformers were fallible; it is only as their witness was supported by the weight of *evangelical tradition* nurtured by the Spirit and the Word that their words have merit today.

Authoritative hermeneutics for the Protestant, and for all believers, is ultimately a quest for God as revealed in God's Son, who is the truth that frees and the power that saves. Neither heteronomous nor autonomous authority is enough; only "theonomous" authority, the name of God as expressed on the lips of Jesus the Christ, will satisfy. Since the ability to be in an equal relationship with either God or Jesus is not presently possible, the Protestant is dependent upon the scriptural interpretation of revelation and the current activity of the Holy Spirit in the life of the church. Such dependence testifies that final certitude is not possible short of God. For many this is the time of waiting in faith; for others it is a time of frustration before proximate authorities.

Baptized Conscience and the Councils

Living, then, between the time of promise and final certitude, what guidelines must the Christian maintain in the interlocking relationship of authority and hermeneutics? The organic interrelationship of authority and hermeneutics will always exist within the church, causing tensions between the magisterium and the charismatic exegete, between the forces for continuity and those for discontinuity, and between the councils of the past and the conscience of the *laos,* the people of God, in the present. For a charismatic synthesis to emerge, the Christian community must dare to listen to God's Spirit leading through uncharted waters. Only the baptized conscience of the pilgrim will see the Spirit at work guiding the church into tomorrow's tradition.

The present search for unity among the churches is actually a search for common authority. A common authority is dependent upon an ecumenically supported hermeneutic that is authoritative for all Christians. Such an authoritative hermeneutic will affirm the human realities of finitude and freedom. God has sanctioned both our finitude and freedom.

Finitude is the line that divides the creature from the Creator. To cross the line in our quest for authoritative interpretations will lead to falsehood and idolatry, whether in the form of biblicism, papalism, or conciliarism. We must recover the eschatological dimension within all "authoritative interpretations." The organic balance between authority and hermeneutics can be rightly maintained if the *eschatological presence* is not ignored in any interpretative endeavor.

Without this eschatological presence we are in danger of promoting further dogmas that bear no resemblance to the revelation that we are responsible for communicating, not fabricating. The reality of our finitude will constantly probe whether or not we include the eschatological presence essential to the hermeneutical task. The need for an *ecumenical hermeneutic* points also toward an *ecumenical eschatology.* Only as we share in a common hope can we expose our weak fears and dogmas that imprison our spirits and grieve God's Spirit.

The second reality for an ecumenical hermeneutic is the reality of freedom. Freedom is the essential category that makes humans *human* and God *God.* To ignore or neglect the reality of freedom for either humans or God is to abandon the landscape of revelation. Authoritative interpretations in each ecclesiastical community have named heretics whom subsequent history has viewed as pioneers. Our past should remind us of the unending tension between freedom and authority; without such awareness "authoritative interpretations" of Christian life and thought can block the truth. For the believer, Nicholas Berdyaev asserts, "the Freedom of the spirit is, inwardly and ideally speaking, prior to authority. . . . Liberty is at once more original than authority, for the origin of the latter is in liberty. The seat of authority is not in the object but in the subject. Authority means one of two things; it is either our free acceptance of a certain principle, or else the enslavement of the spirit."[5]

Berdyaev, speaking from his Eastern Orthodox background, has rightly commented that

> there are no compelling and material proofs of religious truths, nor can there be any. The criterion is in ourselves, not outside. The authority of Ecumenical Councils which are the source of Orthodox faith also demand our individual sanction, our own acts of freedom and of faith, as well as our spiritual life and experience. An Ecumenical Council is not true for me unless it is an inward occurrence of my own spiritual world, that is, an experience lived out in me and in the inmost depths of my spirit. A Council, insofar as it is simply a projection upon the outward historical plane, has only a secondary and reflected significance. Nothing possesses authority for me save that which is recognized as truth in my own spiritual world, as a genuine contact with primary reality having its origin in the primordial freedom of my spirit.[6]

Any form of authority or authoritative interpretation that denies us our freedom also denies us our humanity. The baptized conscience led by the Spirit will not let us forget the twin realities of finitude and freedom as we seek *reliable* interpretations of the Gospel for our day.

Berdyaev's particular understanding of authority on which he bases his spirituality does not harmonize with traditional Eastern Orthodox understanding of authority.[7] Orthodoxy views authority in Christocentric terms, which is to say that authority is viewed as a gift from the Father to the Son and from the Son to the apostles. According to Bishop Kallistos, "Christ exercises his authority above all in three ways: by casting out evil spirits (Luke 4:36; cf. Mark 1:27), by teaching (Matt. 7:29; Mark 1:22), and by forgiving sins (Matt. 9:6; Mark 2:10; Luke 5:24)."[8] This Christocentric model of authority is shared, then, with the apostles, who in turn become leaders for the early church. In time, this authority was entrusted to bishops in each locale by virtue of their succession from the apostles. When bishops gather together collectively by means of an Ecumenical Council they are empowered to speak for the whole church everywhere. The council represented by bishops is an ecclesiastical authority that defines dogma under the inspiration and guidance of the Holy Spirit. From this traditional Orthodox perspective on authority, Berdyaev's view may seem to be too individualistic and subjective. Yet, both Berdyaev and the bishops at council are each in their own way in agreement; namely, a common dependence on the Holy Spirit is needed for guidance. Some find this guidance through heightened spirituality as in the prayers of interiority that we examine in the next chapter.

5

Empowering Theology:
The Prayers of
Interiority

> What we need to do ultimately in the study of religion is to
> break down that simplified opposition between learning *about*
> religion and feeling the living power of religion. The two can
> go together and indeed must go together if the study of reli-
> gion is to enter boldly into its new era of promise.
> —Ninian Smart,
> *The Science of Religion and Sociology of Knowledge*

Substitute the word "theology" for "religion" in the above quotation and
we are faced with the primary dilemma confronting thinking Christians
today. How do we study theology without losing the living power it
wishes to express? How do we synthesize learning and feeling, theologizing and spiritualizing? Are we able to experience the spiritual reality
of our theology as we conceptualize it before others? Or are we drown-
ing in a sea of abstraction and ambiguities? Is the underlying sickness in
contemporary theology the apparent lack of experience within ourselves
of the very theology about which we talk and write? Is the theologian's
apparent lack of experiential knowledge of the transcendent the missing
note in today's theologizing?

We are all aware that the discipline of theology is in search of its own
identity. Much has already been written on the subject.[1] Every theologian seems to have a clue to what is missing.

There does seem to be consensus that the era of "theological giants"
is now over. We have shifted from the systematic *Summas* to the bio-
graphic, shorter, pithy style associated with the Pauline epistles and Pascal's *Pensées*. In contrast, there are also attempts to construct abstract
philosophical theologies in David Tracy's *Blessed Rage for Order* and Edward Farley's *Ecclesial Man*. The latter two works are concerned with

establishing criteria for attempting meaningful theologizing. I have personally been enlightened and stimulated by these studies, but neither Tracy's revisionist model nor Farley's phenomenological approach will be the panacea for the future. There hangs a cloud of suspicion over Christian theologians today; we are suffering from a loss of reality at the very heart of theologizing. As Edward Farley so incisively asks,

> Could it be that there are no realities at all behind the language of this historical faith? Could it be that the testimony, the storytelling, the liturgical expressions of this faith refer to entities that have only phenomenal status? Could it be that the mode of human existence which this historical religion calls faith involves no cognizing, no apprehendings, at all? Are Christian theologians like stockbrokers who distribute stock certificates on a nonexistent corporation? In this situation, the "reality" of the corporation, its size, type, power, and promise, turns out to be simply the broker himself.[2]

How are we to regain reality in the midst of our verbiage? David Tracy outlines for us a course of action grounded in methodological reflection, which he prefers to call "fundamental theology." This approach is similar, although not identical, to the traditional "apologetic" task of theology.[3] Tracy's aim is to determine the criteria needed for theological reasoning. Tracy understands the task of fundamental theology as the attempt to clarify norms and procedures, methods and rules of evidence, upon which serious and meaningful theologizing can take place. Tracy is realistically aware that establishing criteria per se for theological argument will not by itself restore integrity and vitality to the theological enterprise. Tracy calls for a joint effort from all the disciplines of the theological faculty—fundamental, historical, biblical, systematic, and practical. A team effort in theologizing is certainly needed, but I am disappointed to see Tracy's uncritical acceptance of the present territorial divisions within our theological faculties. These curricular divisions have also contributed, I believe, to the fragmented state of today's theological enterprise, destroying the possibility of wholeness within the theological community.

This fragmentation of theological studies has been responsible in part for the numerous "theologies of . . ." that have mushroomed in recent years. Many have contributed to this mushrooming effect by their frantic wish to plug the dikes of doubt and suspicion in the midst of ambiguity. Others have fostered these ad hoc theologies in a search for relevance without taking a realistic assessment of the complex marketplace. As a result, theologians have become theologically bankrupt, with almost no influence beyond the halls of our theological ghettos. We no longer find ourselves articulate witnesses to the sense of transcendence; our past experiences have been depleted of all content without being replenished. When, at times, we find a colleague with a recent experience of divine encounter, we are more suspicious than grateful. As a consequence, we have created distance between ourselves and the vitality of the biblical witness to the power of the living God. We have been too preoccupied with talking about theology without experiencing the Subject of our theologizing. What we need is a new spirituality to unite with our theologizing.

It is possible for us to have new encounters with the living God if we are willing to recover *the practice of interiority* within the heart of our theologizing process. We cannot afford to leave the practice of interiority solely to monks, spiritualists, Eastern gurus, New Age religionists, and transcendental meditation practitioners. We must recover the practice of interiority that is at the center of our Christian texts and traditional experience. Theologian Mary McDermott Shideler is correct in observing that theological circles, unfortunately, are paying little attention to mystical and ascetic theologies and practices.[4] *Is this inattention the missing factor needed in revitalizing contemporary theology?* Perhaps our need is not a revisionist theology à la Tracy, but a recovery of interiority within the theologizing process. Perhaps we can learn from the forms of interiority in practice today.

For the purpose of this limited discussion, we will look at two practices of interiority found in hesychasm and transcendental meditation. The latter has enjoyed wide coverage through the media, while the former is better known to students of Eastern Christianity. Can either of these approaches to interiority contribute to the theological task?

Hesychasm: Past and Present

Hesychasm is an internalized method of theologizing through prayer, associated with Byzantine monasticism. The ultimate aim is a mystical union with God within a context of silence. The Greek word *hesychia* means tranquillity or peace. Ultimate tranquillity is a state of silence or quietude. Achieving this silence is difficult; however, the result is a convergence of thought and feeling in the theologizing process in the form of a listening prayer. In an article about the Jesus Prayer, Kallistos Ware said the hesychast, "the person who has attained *hesychia,* inward stillness or silence, is *par excellence* the one who listens. He listens to the voice of prayer in his own heart, and understands that this voice is not his own but that of Another speaking within him."[5] Theologizing that stems from this prayer event was described by Saint Gregory Palamas (1296–1359) as a "theology of facts" pointing to the following demonstrable realities—God's freedom, will, and action in the individual. A theology of facts is based upon experience and nurtured in prayer.

The hesychast traces the tradition of such prayerful theologizing to the example of Jesus in the desert wilderness, and later in the church fathers—Gregory of Nyssa, Dionysius, Maximus, Basil, and Origen. The tradition was continued among great monastic figures such as Barsanuphius and Dorotheus of Gaza, Diadochus of Photike, John Climacus and his *Leader of Paradise*, Macarius of Egypt and Macarius of Alexandria, Evagrius of Pontus, Arsenius the Great, and Symeon the New Theologian.

Symeon (949–1022) stands as the greatest of the Byzantine mystics. His mystical vision of divine and uncreated light took Byzantine tradition a step further in its understanding of the mysterious world of transcendence. His vision was likened to the event experienced by the disciples who saw Jesus surrounded by light at his transfiguration on Mount Tabor. Byzantine theology had to wait for more than three centuries until Gregory Palamas synthesized this mystical vision of the hesychast into the Byzantine apophatic doctrine of God.

How to obtain such a mystical experience was described in particular by Nicephorus the Hesychast, whose *Method of Holy Prayer and Attention* is attributed to either Symeon the New Theologian or to Gregory of Sinai (1255–1346).[6] The latter was a contemporary of Gregory Palamas; the two had overlapping periods of residence on Mount Athos, but there is no record of any direct contact between them. Gregory of Sinai was noted as the teacher and guide into deeper mysteries of hesychastic prayer life, while Palamas was the apologist and theologian of hesychasm, defending it against attacks from Barlaam, the Italo-Greek Calabrian.

Gregory of Sinai taught and practiced the hesychastic life in the semieremitic milieu of a secluded *skete* on Mount Athos. He surrounded himself with chosen disciples. With his group and individually Gregory explored the meaning and implication of the Pauline exhortation "pray without ceasing" (1 Thess. 5:17, KJV). This Pauline command was obviously not limited to secluded monks but applied to all Christians. Gregory is known to have told one of his disciples, Isidore (later a patriarch), not to remain on Athos, but to return to Thessalonika and there guide a circle of lay people in the practice of urban hesychasm. Gregory viewed inner prayer as a possibility in the city as well as in some isolated mountain spot; for him mysticism and society were not necessarily incompatible or mutually exclusive.[7]

"Pray without ceasing" for the Eastern Christian is essentially an attitude of contemplation and interiority which centers on the heart. When Orthodox writers speak of the "prayer of the heart," they are referring to one particular prayer, *the Jesus Prayer*. It consists of the constant repetition of the name "Jesus." Through the years the Invocation of the Name was incorporated into a short sentence known as "the Jesus Prayer":

> Lord Jesus Christ, Son of God, have mercy on me.

The above sentence also has variations:

> Lord Jesus Christ, Son of God, have mercy on me a sinner.
> Lord Jesus Christ, have mercy on me.
> Son of God, have mercy on me.
> Jesus, Son of God, have mercy on me.
> Lord Jesus Christ, save me.
> Master Jesus, protect me.
> Jesus, help me.[8]

The Eastern Orthodox Christian has interpreted "pray without ceasing" to mean that the Jesus Prayer should reside in the heart, collecting the thoughts and feelings of the believer into a unit of wholeness and union with God. In order to acquire the true prayer of the heart, the mind must be unified. It must move from fragmentation to singleness, from plurality to simplicity and even nakedness in order to enter and dwell within the heart. This is the goal of the Jesus Prayer.[9] To enhance the process, repetition of the Jesus Prayer came to be associated with certain physical exercises designed to improve concentration. Breathing was carefully regulated in tune with the prayer. Gregory of Sinai instructed his disciples as follows:

> From early morning sit down on a low stool, about eight inches; compress your mind, forcing it down from your brain into your heart, and keep it there. Laboriously bow yourself down, feeling sharp pain in your chest, shoulders and neck, and cry persistently in mind and soul, "Lord Jesus Christ, have mercy on me." Then, because of the constraint and labour, and also perhaps because of the feeling of distaste that results from this continual effort—but not, certainly, for he says, "they who feed on me

55

shall still be hungry" (Ecclus 24:21)—transfer your mind to the second half and say, "Son of God, have mercy on me." Repeat this many times, and do not from laziness change frequently from one half to the other: for trees which are continually transplanted do not grow roots. Control the drawing in of your breath, so that you do not breathe at your ease. For the current of air which rises from the heart darkens the mind and agitates the intelligence, keeping it far from the heart. . . . Hold back the expulsion of your breath, so far as possible, and enclose your mind in your heart, continually and persistently practicing the invocation of the Lord Jesus.[10]

The above description of praying and breathing together has been called the "hesychast method of prayer." The hesychast realizes an interrelationship between this physical technique of breathing and inner psychic and spiritual activity. The novice in this technique usually has a teacher. Learning to control and regulate physical processes is to enhance inward concentration in prayer. The method consists of three major aspects. (1) External posture of the body: the person assumes an uncomfortable position. (2) Control of breathing: the person learns to breathe slowly in coordination with the rhythm of the Jesus Prayer.[11] Often the first part of the prayer ("Lord Jesus Christ, Son of God") is said while drawing in the breath, and the second part ("have mercy on me, a sinner") while breathing out. Variations on this rhythm are used. The Jesus Prayer may also be synchronized with the beating of the heart. (3) Inward exploration: "Just as the aspirant in Yoga is taught to concentrate his thought in specific parts of his body," Timothy Ware says, "so the Hesychast concentrates his thought in the cardiac center. While inhaling through his nose and propelling his breath down into his lungs, he makes his mind 'descend' with the breath and he 'searches' inwardly for the place of the heart."[12] Directions for this inward exploration are not committed to writing, hence the need for a teacher to guide the novice on the spiritual journey. The hesychast also seeks to keep free from all images and objects of human imagination. The target of the prayer is the heart. For the Eastern Christian, the heart signifies the center of a person, the individual's interior face turned toward God. The body constitutes the exterior face of the human being. The heart is the interior mirror where the believer confronts joys and frustrations. The heart is the conscience, where temptations are encountered and inner struggles are fought.[13] The heart is also the residence of the spirit and soul of the individual. In short, since the heart is the center of a person, the believer needs to attain purity of heart through prayer. From this standpoint, we can better understand the importance the hesychast attaches to the beatitude, "Blessed are the pure in heart, for they shall see God" (Matt. 5:8). The experience of transcendence, the encounter with God, is given only to the "pure in heart."

Orthodox writers on hesychasm insist that the essence of prayer is not linked to breathing exercises or body position. These are simply aids to concentration, useful to individuals in varying degrees. The hesychasts are well aware "that there can be no mechanical means of acquiring God's grace, and no techniques leading automatically to the mystical state," Ware writes in *The Orthodox Church*.[14] The weight of the hesychast approach should be placed upon its understanding of prayer. For Gregory of Sinai, prayer is God. Prayer in the deepest and fullest sense is God's action in us through the Holy Spirit. Gregory considers the essence of prayer to be our incorporation into God's plan manifested in our baptism. Baptism is God's act of grace within us. Prayer is the discovery and disclosure of this baptismal grace; through the name of Jesus the baptismal grace is reenacted within us. "Our aim in the life of prayer," according to Gregory, "is to bring to light this divine presence within us, to remove the obstacles of sin so that the grace of Baptism may become fully 'active' in our heart. Prayer, then, is to become what we already are, to gain what we already possess, to come face to face with the one who dwells even now within our innermost self."[15]

The objective of an ascetic and of mystical theology is found within the sacrament of baptism. Through ascetic effort (simplified life-style, body position, and breathing) and through the repetition of the Jesus Prayer, the meaning and experience of baptism (and the living presence of the indwelling Godhead symbolized by the baptism) are rediscovered and actualized in the believer. To reach this mystical understanding of baptismal grace, the hesychast must live a disciplined and simple life. Gregory of Sinai suggests the following daily regimen in reaching for this sublime level of interiority and communion with the living God:

> *By day:*
> Hour 1: the "memory of God," prayer (i.e., the Jesus Prayer), "quiet of the heart."
> Hour 2: reading
> Hour 3: *psalmodia* (recitation of the Psalter)

The same three activities are prescribed in the same sequence for the fourth, fifth, and sixth hours and for the seventh, eighth, and ninth hours. As an alternative to this threefold sequence, Gregory suggests that the Jesus Prayer may be used without interruption.

Hour 10: meal
Hour 11: sleep (if desired)
Hour 12: vespers

By night: Here three possibilities are specified.

(i) *Beginners:* One half of the night is to be spent in vigil and the other half in sleep. Midnight forms the point of division, but it does not matter whether the sleep or the vigil comes first.

(ii) *Intermediaries (mesoi,* "those in the middle"): four hours of sleep and eight of vigil, arranged thus:

one to two hours awake (? spent in recitation of the Jesus Prayer)

four hours asleep

six hours awake, spent in prayer: Matins (*Orthros*) with the reading of the Psalter and prayer (presumably the Jesus Prayer); then Prime.

(iii) *The Perfect:* These, says Gregory, keep vigil standing without interruption throughout the whole night![16]

As the hesychast was engaged in the daily discipline of prayer, Gregory Palamas was fighting to justify the mystical experience of the hesychast within Byzantine tradition. Palamas was victorious over his challengers, particularly Barlaam, and hesychasm was accepted within Byzantine theology. Palamas through his efforts identified three basic themes of Eastern Christian spirituality and theology: (1) theology as apophatic in character; (2) revelation as light; and (3) salvation as deification.

For Palamas, all Christians (not only monks) have access to the deifying power of grace. This knowledge of God is an experience given to all believers. Meyendorff, summarizing Palamas, states, "In Christ, God assumed the whole of man, soul and body; and man as such was deified. In prayer—for example, in the 'method'—in the sacraments, in the entire life of the Church as a community, man is called to participation in divine life: this participation is also the true knowledge of God."[17] The Christian life was a summons to holiness and love in Christ. For Palamas, Jaroslav Pelikan says, the message of salvation was a "disclosure of authentic humanity, as purification, as the conjunction of divine and human, and above all, as deification—patristic ideas all, but synthesized into what must be called a 'new theology.'"[18] In short, salvation was more than forgiveness for Palamas; it was the genuine renewal of the individual.

Palamas insisted that all believers should have not only a knowledge of God (*gnosis*) but union with God (*enosis*). Since God is totally inaccessible in essence, the believer through the process of deification (*theosis*) can become "God" by grace or energy. This renewal of the individual is not achieved through human effort, but by the "energies" of God, who beckons the individual into communion with the Divine Nature. It is within the summit of this communion that one experiences the light (the revelation) of Mount Tabor. Palamas claimed this was a "theology of fact" that transcended all psychic or mystical experiences achieved outside of grace. Thus Palamas saw the phenomenon of light as a factual and nonsymbolic revelation from God. God's energies take the form of light; this was a theological fact for Palamas. However, the essence of God remained unknown, thus maintaining the traditional apophatic theology of the early church fathers. As Meyendorff explained, "The energies, therefore, are never considered as divine emanations, or as a diminished God. They are divine life, as given by God to His creatures; and they are God, for in His Son He truly gave Himself for our salvation."[19] Thus Palamas was able to build a theological case in which the hesychast method was an acceptable means of enabling the believer to experience *theosis*. Deification brought one's true humanity to the surface. For the hesychast, an individual can be truly human only when a mystical reunion takes place with God through Christ.

For all the hesychasts, participation in the divine light came to be regarded as the apotheosis of mystical experience. For Symeon, Gregory of Sinai, and Palamas, this revelation of God as light and deification as salvation were all to be seen within a christological context. The vision of light does not constitute the goal of mystical experience. The ultimate end of the Jesus Prayer is to make the divine presence known and to stand in communion with the Lord in the light. This communion is made possible through the Holy Spirit, who converses and operates in the heart of the believer, leading ultimately to an empirical experience of Christ as a person. Listen to the testimony of Symeon following his own mystical ecstasy through hesychasm:

> When I desired to see Thee again, and once went to the immaculate ikon of her who gave birth to Thee, to salute it and fall down before it, Thou didst appear to me before I stood up, in my suffering heart making it like light. And then I knew that I consciously possessed Thee in me. From that moment I no longer loved Thee and Thy properties as a re-

membrance, in their memory only, but I believed that I had Thee truly in me, O Personal and Essential Love, for Thou art the real Love, O God.[20]

Many of the experiences of the hesychasts are found in the great encyclopedia of Eastern piety, the *Philokalia.* From these writings there emerges the ethical and practical piety of the Eastern Christian tradition. The *Philokalia* is treasured by every devout believer. Such was the case of an unknown nineteenth-century Russian pilgrim who wrote of his experiences as he wandered throughout the land with his copy of the *Philokalia,* saying the Jesus Prayer.

> At times I do as much as forty-three miles a day, and do not feel that I am walking at all. I am aware only of the fact that I am saying my Prayer. When the bitter cold pierces me, I begin to say my Prayer more earnestly and I quickly get warm all over. When hunger begins to overcome me, I call more often on the Name of Jesus, and I forget my wish for food. When I fall ill and get rheumatism in my back and legs, I fix my thoughts on the Prayer and do not notice the pain. If anyone harms me I have only to think, "How sweet is the Prayer of Jesus!" and the injury and the anger alike pass away and I forget it all. I have become a sort of half-conscious person. I have no cares and no interests. The fussy business of the world I would not give a glance to. The one thing I wish for is to be alone, and all by myself to pray, to pray without ceasing; and doing this, I am filled with joy.[21]

The account of the pilgrim's journey found its way into J. D. Salinger's novel *Franny and Zooey,* which brought the Jesus Prayer to the attention of many in the West. As Franny became bored and disgusted with the excessive materialism around her, she found comfort in her "pea-green covered book," *The Way of a Pilgrim.* It gave her an entirely new perspective on her present life. In the Prayer, she attempts to find a meaningful encounter with the realm of the spirit. She wishes to escape from the material world of uncertainty and meaninglessness. She believes the Jesus Prayer to be a mechanical, sure way of running away from the world of selfishness and heartless competition.[22] But Franny was mistaken at one crucial point, according to George Maloney. "She was wrong in thinking of the Jesus Prayer as an automatic means of escaping God's created world in order to retire into an interior world of the spirit where there would be only certainty and beauty unending. Only at the end of the novel through the help of her brother, Zooey, she understands that Christian prayer cannot be used as an escape from God's world nor can the Jesus Prayer be used by one who has not encountered Jesus Christ in an experiential knowledge of who he is."[23]

Perhaps Zooey had read Gregory of Sinai or Palamas, who concur with this view of the Prayer.

The search for interiority in today's marketplace is motivated by a quest, similar to Franny's, for escape from the struggles and stresses of contemporary society. Our affluency and technology have led us to expect instant solutions. What is needed is an inner quest for silence—an urban hesychasm that does not ignore the social responsibilities around us.

One form of urban hesychasm is found in "centering prayer," inspired by Thomas Merton, perhaps the best known of our twentieth-century monks. Merton discovered early in his life the importance of interiority, influenced as he was by the patristic texts and the hesychast tradition. He emphasized that the primary way to experience the living God is to focus on one's center and from there to pass into God.

Centering prayer can take place whenever a person is comfortably settled in a good chair and relaxed. Centering involves the following procedure:

> *Step one:* At the beginning take a minute or two to quiet down as you journey inward in faith to the depth of your being and to God who is at the center of your being.
>
> *Step two:* Pick a single familiar word that is meaningful for you and repeat it as you rest at the center of your being in God's faith-filled love.
>
> *Step three:* Whenever you are distracted during your quiet contemplation, gently return to the Lord through the simple repeating of your prayer word.[24]

It is generally advised that centering prayer be practiced for a twenty-minute period twice a day. As the centering experience concludes each time, the person is encouraged to take a few minutes to withdraw slowly from the deep state of contemplation and to end by saying the prayer common to all Christians, "Our Father." Such moments of contemplation hold the possibility of reevaluating involvements and empowering theological reflections in our discipleship under God.

A contemporary theology sensitized by a process of interiority might provide the necessary perspective to transcend our excessive preoccupation with self. Harvey Cox has suggested the need for "a rebirth of the monastic movement in which the monasteries are co-ed and are also cities."[25] Cox may be right. There is a growing sense of the need for community and interiority within our lives. He correctly observes that "the mystics and contemplatives have served as the guardians and explorers of that uniquely human realm called 'interiority.' I think we need them today, perhaps more than we ever have, precisely because authentic personal life is now so fatally threatened by an intrusive technical world."[26]

Our response has been a "consciousness revolution" searching for inner peace through Zen, Yoga, New Age, psychosynthesis, est, bioenergetics, Arica, biofeedback, Silva Mind Control, Feldenkrais Method, and meditation. Does this renaissance of interiority represent an instinct for survival by the jostled and threatened human spirit?

Transcendental Meditation: An Update on an Ancient Practice

Transcendental meditation may be viewed as one of the forerunners introducing today's far-ranging expressions of New Age religious consciousness. Known to countless thousands as TM, its neatly packaged solution might be seen as an abbreviated form of hesychasm. The mantra, a secret Sanskrit word, may be viewed as a substitute for the Jesus Prayer. This, however, is where the similarity begins and ends between these two practices of interiority. Each operates within a different metaphysics. The teachers of TM emphasize its therapeutic side, minimizing its metaphysical dimensions. TM is presented primarily as a practical discipline and its religious tradition is minimized. TM is promoted as a "scientific" means or technique for transforming and renewing persons to a higher level of vigor and well-being.

TM, like Merton's centering, calls for two periods (each approximately twenty minutes) of meditation per day, and when properly executed, it promises a new consciousness and source of refreshment and relief for persons under stress in their daily routines. TM has been enthusiastically adopted by many in the business and professional community. Today it is claimed there are an estimated one million meditators in the United States. These meditators are taught meditation through the use of a mantra, the word selected for them by their TM teacher at the conclusion of a brief course.

The mantra is repeated silently by the meditator as a means of emptying the mind and relaxing the autonomic nervous system. The mantra itself is taken from a version of Vedantic spirituality, a monotheistic form of Hinduism in which adherents aspire to unite with an absolute being. Maharishi Mahesh Yogi, the founder of TM, claimed that the mantra has no meaning for the meditator other than the value of the sound. The mantra is a tool for thinking, one that enables the individual to regulate the state of consciousness.

Waking, sleeping, and dreaming are the three recognized states of consciousness. This fourth or meditation state is called by Robert Keith Wallace of the Maharishi International University "a wakeful, hypometabolic physiologic state." Tests performed by Wallace show that a wakeful state of meditation actually lowers metabolism and thus reduces stress. His experimental findings have been challenged by scientists, including Herbert Benson, a cardiologist and faculty member at the Harvard Medical School. Benson, an early collaborator with Wallace, disagreed with Wallace's findings in later research, pointing out that TM has no monopoly on meditation. According to Benson, other mental techniques and approaches can be used to bring about the results of reduced stress and relaxation. He calls his own approach "Relaxation Response."[27]

The major testimony out of the TM movement is that *meditation works*. The Maharishi Mahesh Yogi sought to expand on the benefits of this experience through "the benefits of the Technology of the Unified Field." He wrote in the preface of the Maharishi International University Bulletin for 1990–92:

> The specialty of the teaching procedure at MIU is that every lesson is connected with the common source of all lessons, the field of total knowledge of that discipline; and that in turn is connected with the common source of all disciplines, the field of pure intelligence of the students themselves. In this way, as the students gain knowledge of different disciplines, automatically they awaken more and more to the reality of the creative potential of their own intelligence. They realize that all fields of knowledge are the different modes of their own intelligence, the unified field of all the laws of nature.

A complete copy of his statement and related materials on TM can be had by writing to MIU in Fairfield, Iowa.[28] The Maharishi's statement does not imply that transcendental meditation increases "creative intelligence" in terms of creative products or raised IQ, but rather that "the unified field of all the laws of nature" will improve one's outlook and perception of the world and people. The fourth or transcendent state of consciousness enables the meditator to go beyond transient thoughts and reach for the very source of thought.[29] This suggests a disguised metaphysics, an interpretative handle to the nature of reality. It is precisely at this point that TM reaches beyond the boundary of "technique" and unveils its philosophic and religious tradition. This is not necessarily bad; in fact, it may be necessary if TM is to survive as something more substantial than a faddish technique. In the highly competitive world of gurus, its earlier popularity among persons in the business community may be declining.

Sources for
Contemporary Theology?

A series of questions at the beginning of this study were concerned with the state and health of the theological task. Each theologian is searching for the missing factor or factors in today's theologizing process. This discussion has raised the issue of whether the practice of interiority seen in hesychasm, transcendental meditation, or other forms of centering is a possible source useful to the contemporary theologian. Two of these practices of interiority have been examined briefly from this perspective. Can hesychasm and TM help theologians to synthesize creatively the rational and nonrational dimensions of theology? My own answer is a *qualified yes* to hesychasm. At the same time I find no need for transcendental meditation since its benefits are already available through hesychasm and other forms of Christian meditation. My limited approval of hesychasm is as follows:

1. A disciplined practice of interiority in the theologizing process is a prerequisite to successfully synthesizing our thoughts and feelings. Hesychasm is a reminder of this fact and has its own technique for interiorization leading to a state of silent communion with the Sacred. This "quiet time" on a regular basis provides the solitude needed in a noisy culture. Most of us sense this, but neglect the practice of solitude for one reason or another. As Sam Keen has observed for himself, "I have fled from solitude, seeking comfort in the arms of a woman, the company of friends or the applause of the public."[30] These comforts are needed, but the need for solitude is equally urgent. Hesychasm reminds us of the significance of solitude in recovering the Sacred.

2. The hesychast techniques for reaching interiority do not inspire me. Body posture, breath control, the Jesus Prayer (as mantra) can lead not only to altered states of consciousness and change in phys-

ical chemistry, but also in the end to nothing more than an empty, mechanical spirituality. The hesychasts are aware of this danger; in fact, they have been accused of being Euchites or Messalians— praying people who have turned their praying into a fetish. The techniques of interiority can be deceptive tools resulting in super-ficial experiences, not truly an encounter with the living God.

3. The emphasis of the Jesus Prayer is upon the *Kyrie Eleison* ("Lord have mercy"). This is good biblical theology. Who is not in need daily of forgiving and being forgiven? Who is not in need of re-ceiving mercy? The theologian has a powerful message at this point, in a society that has lost its understanding of forgiveness and its capacity to practice it. Furthermore, the *Kyrie Eleison* reminds us that God is encountered not as a postulate or proposition, but as an experienced fact. Contemporary theology has lost its capacity to relate such "factual" experiences. The *Kyrie Eleison* also prompts us to shift from a dispassionate observer's stance in our theologizing to one of personal involvement in which feelings and thoughts can be freely expressed and integrated into a totality that makes us responsible participants as we theologize.

4. The interiorization process, as illustrated especially through hesy-chasm, can help us to transcend the middle-class entrapments in which most of us practice theology. The ascetic approach within hesychasm can awaken us to our spiritual inability to cope with affluence. This inability within our ranks has left the predominant role of leadership to others in the marketplace.

An ascetic theology can be a theology of simplicity incarnate. This became very clear to me in a lengthy taped interview with a Trappist monk, a semi-hermit practicing hesychasm. His life-style and beliefs are an eloquent testimony of the transcendent realities witnessed within the Christian faith. Personally, I am not about to leave my wife and family and emulate this Trappist monk! How-ever, his hesychast style communicated to me a meaningful en-counter with transcendence. Perhaps theologians in particular should plan for short-term sabbatical leaves as experienced by Henri J. M. Nouwen, who took a leave to enter a Trappist Mon-astery in Genesee, New York.[31] Such experiences may help us to recover a measure of mystique and credibility in our theologizing process. This is especially important if we continue to become a society of "psychonauts" navigating through "inner space." An as-cetic and mystical dimension to our theologizing may enable us to acquire "new eyes and new ears" to discover the transcendent realities before us.

5. Finally, hesychasm underlines for us a truth long recognized by the early Greek theologians and later adopted by Karl Marx that "practice is the basis of theory."[32] The task of theology is not simply to interpret to the world but also to change it. The aim of theologizing is praxis. The practice of Christian devotion will unfold a nearness with God and evoke a loving response and heightened commitment to God and to the *imago dei* in all persons. Hesychasts and meditators must avoid the temptation to limit themselves to the experience of ecstasy.

Mother Teresa is right: "prayer without action is nothing."[33] The newly acquired vision of God must in turn motivate us to reach out to the oppressed with compassion and with the courage to assist them in the process of changing and humanizing societal structures. This is what Gregory of Sinai encouraged by sending his young disciple from Athos to practice urban hesychasm. Unfortunately, most groups in today's "consciousness revolution," including TM, seem to be overly preoccupied with self-concern and self-actualization. These consciousness seekers can learn from the early monastic communities. These communities were designed as models or centers of renewal, called upon to practice an ethic of sociospirituality.[34] The Taizé Community is a good example of a monastic community fulfilling a responsible ethic of sociospirituality.

Contemporary theology can indeed learn and be empowered by the prayers of interiority. However, a critical stance should also be assumed before each approach. Some methods can serve in a limited way as a catalyst furthering the theologizing process beyond verbalization to those actual experiences of the living God uttered in the unfolding depths of the *Kyrie Eleison.*

6

Nationalism, Modernization, and Orthodoxy in the Balkans

Not only in the Danube territories of present-day Romania but through-out the Balkans, national and religious self-identity have been intimately linked for centuries. Apart from the common Byzantine heritage of Christians in the Balkans, it is almost impossible to regard the Balkans as a unifiable entity. Geographically the Balkans are the peninsula formed by the Adriatic, Aegean, and Black seas. In practice, the Balkans seem to be a state of mind: namely, tangled, desperate, and divided. In fact "to balkanize" means to divide into small antagonistic states. Today, the Balkan nations have again increased their reputation for explosiveness along with their ambiguity. The key to understanding the Balkans lies in a recognition of the diverse nationalistic aspirations of the peoples in this southeastern region of the European continent. The forces of Balkan nationalism looked upon religion as one significant means of establish-ing their pluralism. Byzantine-Ottoman rule was more interested in con-trol than nationalistic aspirations. The cautious drive for nationhood was an integrally important step toward maturity in the Balkans. National-ism in turn had a significant influence upon the formation of nationally oriented ecclesiastical institutions in the Balkans.

The Phanariots

For the past five hundred years, the religious situation in the Balkans has been one of foreign subjection. Ottoman and Byzantine captivity (the latter was exemplified by the Patriarchate of Constantinople) ran con-currently from the fall of Constantinople to the end of the nineteenth century, climaxed by the Balkan wars of 1912–13. During the seven-teenth century, a particular group of families increasingly dominated the central organization of "the Great Church," as the Greeks fondly called the Orthodox Patriarchate of Constantinople. Referring to themselves as the elite of the Greek nation, this corps of families claimed a high Byzantine ancestry. Because they built homes in the Phanar quarter of Constantinople, in order to be close to the patriarch and his court, these families came to be known as "Phanariots."[1]

To further fortify their position within the Ottoman Empire, the Phanariots extended their influence through wealth, position, and heritage upon the Danube territories. These territories, the Principalities of Wallachia and Moldavia now collectively called Romania, enjoyed self-governing privileges while acknowledging the suzerainty of the sultan. The princes of this region looked favorably upon the Greek Phanariots, and a period of mutual self-interest and cross-cultural influence began.

Flushed with economic success, the Phanariots learned well the lesson of cooperation with the Ottoman government, becoming the leading bankers, financiers, and physicians of the empire. Wishing to consolidate these gains within the limits set by the Turks, the Phanariots looked for land in which they could invest their wealth and which eventually might provide the basis for rebuilding Byzantium. The Phanariots saw themselves as preservers of Byzantium's glory. The Danube territories presented themselves as an excellent way to realize these dreams. The Danube territories were governed by princes who saw themselves as the heirs of the Byzantine caesars. Hence their ambitions in this direction disposed them to look favorably upon the Phanariots with their enormous wealth and connections with the sultan through the patriarchate. This position of mutual self-interest resulted in a number of significant marriages between the princes and Phanariots.

The apparent advantage of self-government of Wallachia and Moldavia within the Ottoman Empire is debatable. Unlike the neighboring areas of Serbia, Bulgaria, Greece, or Hungary, these territories were free of Turks. No Turkish pasha was sent to govern the Principalities; there were no Turkish magistrates in their law courts, no Turkish landowners, and no mosques on their landscape. More important, the local administrators were people from the area, even though it was known that the heads of government under the Phanariots were exacting a heavy price for this local autonomy. During the gloomiest era of the Phanariots, at the end of the seventeenth and into the eighteenth century, excessive tributes were demanded from the people by the rulers. In turn, the Phanariot appointees had to pay excessive and frequent tributes for their nominations from the sultan. Indirectly, the Turks through the regulation of tributes and other bribes exercised an absentee presence within the Principalities. Within the span of a hundred plus years there were thirty-eight appointees for Wallachia and thirty-five for Moldavia, an average term of less than three years.

This constant change in government in the Principalities had a disastrous effect on the region. Instead of furthering the vision of Byzantium as initially intended by the Phanariots, the Greek nobles appointed to the Principalities actually widened the cleavage between the incoming Byzantine cultural heritage and the local native tradition. The Romanians came to look upon the Phanariots, not as fellow Orthodox, but as a foreign ruling caste who placed economic interests above the spiritual and cultural concerns of Byzantium. The Phanariots, for instance, showed no interest in furthering the art that had developed from Byzantino-Bulgarian roots under the professional guidance of priests and monks. Thus icon painting passed from the "professional" to the peasants who created a new folk art. The Phanariots, as transmitters of Byzantium's glories, failed to gain the necessary grass-roots following. Not only the Wallachians and Moldavians but also the Greeks were victimized by their non-Christian overlords, the Turks.

All was not bad under the Phanariots. Occasional wise rulers, such as Constantine Mavrocordat in Wallachia and Gregory M. Ghica in Moldavia, improved the lot of the peasantry in the eighteenth century. They allowed serfs to purchase liberty from a master or employer by the payment of a sum of money, and set limits to the amounts demanded. Alexander Ypsilanti brought out in 1780, in Greek (the language of administration within the Principalities) and Romanian, a law code for Wallachia that was later adopted in Moldavia. The Phanariots made contributions in education, which also furthered the Byzantium vision within the Principalities. Greek schools and seminaries were founded, notably the academies at Bucharest and Jassy, which supported the general interest of Orthodoxy and not simply hellenization. The Orthodox church in the Principalities was anxious to secure Greek learning and Phanariot money to strengthen itself against Latin missionaries operating from the Hapsburg dominions and from Poland. While the sophisticated clergy were Greek or Greek-educated, the Phanariots did not attempt to change the use of a Slavonic liturgy, replaced in the eighteenth century by the use of the Romanian language.

Nationalization of the Churches

Signs of nationalism were increasing. The patriarchate, through the Phanariots, for instance, was not eager to encourage Romanian separatism. The intention of the patriarchate, married to its Byzantine vision, was to keep the Ottoman Empire intact until such a day that it could be transferred to the Greeks of Constantinople. Hence in the eighteenth century the patriarchate was able to persuade the sultan that he should be given more direct control of the Principalities in order to help preserve the Ottoman Empire, and for the sake of Byzantium to discourage the growing forces of nationalism. The Phanariots in the meantime subjected themselves to all kinds of expense and humiliation vis-à-vis the sultan in order to attain their princely appointments. Why did these wealthy Greeks submit themselves to such costly compromise? Steven Runciman, a noted Byzantine scholar, suggests that the Phanariots did so because the patriarch and his supporting families were chiefly in pursuit of the Imperial idea, the rebirth of Byzantium. "Under Phanariot princes a new-Byzantine culture could find a home in the Principalities. A Greek-born nobility could root itself in lands there; Greek academies could educate citizens for the new Byzantium. There, far better than in the shadowy palaces around the Phanar, with Turkish police at the door, Byzantine ambition could be kept alive. In Romania, in Rum beyond the Danube, the revival of New Rome could be planned."[2] However, as subsequent events in the nineteenth century would show, the push for nationalism would prove to be too much for "the Great Church" and the Phanariots.

Ultimately, the subjection of the patriarchs to their Phanariot benefactors proved to be most costly to the patriarchs themselves—as they slowly surrendered an ecumenical vision of Orthodoxy. The patriarchs' association over the years with the Phanariots identified the primary interests of the Great Church as being more Greek-centered than ecumenical. From the viewpoint of the Wallachians and Moldavians and other national groups in the Balkans, the Great Church under the influence of the Phanariot benefactors was being increasingly managed in the interests of the Greek people at Constantinople, rather than for the benefit of Orthodoxy as a whole.

Since 1453, through an arrangement between the conquering sultan and Patriarch Gennadius, Orthodoxy throughout the Ottoman Empire had been under the authority of the patriarchate. With the passing years, this arrangement came to be less ecumenically administered as the persuasive influences of the key families began to have an impact upon the Phanar district. The Phanariots pushed for tighter Greek control of Orthodoxy throughout the empire. The churches of Wallachia and Moldavia, with their longer history of Greek infiltration, were easier to deal with than the Bulgarians and the Serbs, who had no intention of being Graecized as were the educated clergy in Wallachia and Moldavia. Bulgarians and Serbs protested against the appointment of Greek metropolitans. The Serbian Patriarchate was reconstituted from 1557 to 1755.

The Phanariots were displeased with these reactions and pushed for even greater control, with the approval of the Turks. Runciman reports,

In 1766 the autonomous Metropolitanate of Pec was suppressed and in 1767 the Metropolitanate of Ochrid. The Serbian and Bulgarian Churches were each put under an exarch appointed by the Patriarch. This was the work of the Patriarch Samuel Hantcherli, a member of a rebellious Phanariot family, whose brother Constantine was for a while Prince of Wallachia until his financial extortions alarmed not only the taxpayers but also his ministers, and he was deposed and executed by the Sultan's orders. The exarchs did their best to impose Greek bishops on the Balkan Churches, to the growing anger of both Serbs and Bulgarians. The Serbs recovered their religious autonomy early in the nineteenth century when they won political autonomy from the Turks. The Bulgarian Church had to wait until 1870 before it could throw off the Greek yoke.[3]

The creation in 1877 of the Romanian state, consisting of Wallachia and Moldavia, enabled an independent Romanian Orthodox Church to be so recognized in 1885, and it was declared a patriarchate in 1925. In short, the Phanariot policy of hellenization was doomed to failure, especially in the light of nineteenth-century nationalistic interests. It cost the patriarchate its ecumenical integrity and ultimately denied the Greeks any help from Balkan neighbors in their own fight for independence. The emerging nations of the Balkans had learned to be suspicious of Greek religious rule as well as Turkish political rule, thanks to the Phanariots.

The influence of the Byzantine Phanariots upon Romania, for example, was a mixed blessing, but largely negative. That the Phanariots were not Moslems but Christian rulers was at first warmly welcomed, but then it became clear that the Phanariots were preoccupied with economic interests, status, power, Byzantium, and Orthodoxy in that order. Thus their original motivation for a rebirth of the glories of Byzantium and an ecumenically vital Orthodoxy became subordinated in their own struggle for survival in a grand manner. The Turks capitalized upon the penchant of the Phanariots for security, and the desire of the patriarchs to preserve their church caused Christians to exploit Christians in Romania and throughout the Balkans. Nevertheless, the patriarchs and the Phanariots must be given credit for maintaining a standard of Christian education and witness during the Ottoman Empire. Without the memories of a vibrant faith, even a hellenizing Christian faith, many would have been left with less dignity and self-identity during those centuries of suppression while they awaited the birth of a new spirit. The spirit of nationalism that did emerge gave a new focus to the emotional, religious, and cultural aspirations of the people in the Balkans in their pilgrimage toward maturity.

It was not until the second half of the nineteenth century that the respective national churches in the Balkans began to spin off from the Patriarchate of Constantinople. In 1870, the Church of Bulgaria was declared autocephalous but was not recognized by the Ecumenical Patriarch until 1945 and declared a patriarchate in 1961. The Church in Serbia was organized in 1879 and was recognized as a patriarchate in 1922; the Church in Romania was organized in 1885 and was declared a patriarchate in 1925. In the majority of cases, the Patriarchate of Constantinople relinquished control only reluctantly after initial opposition to the nationally separate Orthodox churches and the creation of new patriarchates. At first, these national churches were accused of being schismatic, practicing the heresy of phyletism—a form of ecclesiastical nationalism. Actually, the earlier Byzantine suppressors of these national churches were in many respects also guilty of phyletism. It is from this period of Ottoman-Byzantine reign that the churches of the Balkans were ushered into the contemporary realities of the twentieth century.

Marxism:
Depressant and Stimulus

With national and ecclesiastical formation well under way, Orthodoxy in the Balkans by the mid-twentieth century was faced with the challenge of Marx-Leninism. Marxism was both a depressant and a stimulus to the churches in the Balkans. Marxism has viewed the church as a vestige of the past, deterring the people from modernization and a higher standard of living. Consequently, Christians (and for that matter Muslims and Jews as well) have suffered much under Marxism, and their activities have been circumscribed by the Marxist governments in the Balkans. Albania, for instance, abolished all institutional religion as such in its desire for maturity and modernization.[4] Romania, instead, decided to cooperate with the church as part of its goal of self-fulfillment.

Romania undoubtedly enjoyed the best relations between church and state. The Orthodox Church of Romania, the quasi-official church that represented 80 percent of the country's twenty-three million people, and the Communist government had a de facto marriage of mutual interest which fostered the nationalistic aims of Romanians. It sometimes startled visitors to see the late President Nicolai Ceauşescu and Patriarch Justinian and his successors present together to greet foreigners. My own experience took place at the Fourteenth International Congress of Byzantine Studies in Bucharest. President Ceauşescu personally and lavishly entertained the delegates to the congress in the stately Palace of Ministry. Present at the presidential reception was Patriarch Justinian. Both the president and the patriarch acknowledged each other's presence properly, thus highlighting the old Byzantine heritage of *symphonia* (harmony) between church and state.

More recently, however, in the context of *perestroika,* Romania's Orthodox church has been criticized for not having protested (and for at times denying) the injustices and lack of freedom under the regime of President Ceauşescu. Certainly many Protestants and Catholics in Romania felt their freedom curtailed during this period. Here is an example of misapplied *symphonia* eclipsing Orthodoxy's prophetic responsibility and faithfulness to truth and justice. In fact, Patriarch Teoctist resigned under pressure in January, 1990, and was later reinstated by the Orthodox synod in April. The World Council of Churches admitted that it, in its wish to be ecumenically supportive of the Romanian Orthodox Church, was mistaken and guilty for not speaking adequately against human rights violations in Romania.[5]

In retrospect, it can be seen that the Romanian Orthodox Church, perhaps the best organized and prosperous of Orthodox churches in the Balkans, paid too high a price in its uncritical support of the state. It is reported that Orthodox clergy continue to receive one-third of their salaries from the government, and this primary church of the country has special status and in turn lends moral support to the programs of modernization and political change in the state. It remains to be seen whether the lessons of the recent past will be ignored by Orthodox leadership.

While atheist clubs continue to exist in Romanian universities, the general mood of the people in the cities and throughout the countryside is an acceptance of ecclesiastical institutions as part of their life-style.

The throngs that attend churches at Easter, it is estimated, involve well over half of the nation's population. Church attendance is also good throughout the year; the numbers are well above the average reported in Western Europe. It is not unusual to find Communist party members, military officers, and youth in attendance among the worshipers. The government has not encouraged new church building, though a few have been built in recent years. Most government funds have been employed in the restoration of historic churches for both nationalistic and tourist considerations. In Bucharest, for example, there are more than two hundred Orthodox churches, which are well attended, but few new churches have been started since World War II even though the population of the city has doubled. Within limitations, then, the church enjoys many unique privileges in Romania, unlike the restrictions experienced by Orthodox churches in other Communist societies. Thus the strange "marriage" between church and state continues to exist in their common goal of a better tomorrow.

My visit to Sofia, Bulgaria, in 1970 revealed that the Orthodox church there had fewer resources than that of the Romanians, but under the late Patriarch Cyril's leadership it sought to maintain its witness among the people. For example, when the state wished to transform the large Monastery of Rila into a national museum in 1961, the leadership of the church led the people in their concern to maintain the monastery. After long discussions, the state reversed its decision and allowed the church to reestablish the monastic life.

In Sofia itself, I recall a bountiful supply of posters and displays announcing the 100th anniversary of Lenin's birth. Lenin's presence was all prevailing on the streets, in the shops and restaurants. Even though his presence is now diminished in the spirit of *perestroika,* that birthday celebration reminded me of the impact Lenin had upon Marxist thought, especially in regard to religion. A look at his emphasis will help us to better understand the environment faced by Christians in the Balkans, where Marxism has been one of the major vehicles through which modernization was introduced. In a collection of Lenin's articles titled *On Religion* there is this exhortation: "We demand that religion be held a private affair so far as the state is concerned. But by no means can we consider religion a private affair so far as our Party is concerned."[6] The latter part of this quote provides the state official with an important loophole to puruse an expedient policy toward the prevailing church in the jurisdiction. This expedient policy has been applied without any uniformity among the several nations in the Balkans.

The dawn of a new era is beginning in the Balkans. Can Orthodoxy in the Balkans expect to be more socially involved in the future? This question is being raised again as the churches experience freedom from restrictions.[7] Since the state has been performing most of the major welfare functions associated earlier with the church, what greater role is there for the church? There is no question that the influence of Marxism prevails, so that religion is seen as a deterrent to progress and modernization. Religion from a Marxist perspective serves as the preserver of the status quo, fosters servility, and is essentially a manipulative factor in the class war among people. In the Marxist society, accordingly, religion has no future. Yet the persistence of religion is an embarrassing dilemma for the Marxists.[8]

One hopes that fresh dialogue may emerge showing all parties concerned that both religion and Marxism share common aims in wishing to humanize society. Marxism and Christianity, for instance, are both revolutionary in spirit. Each in its own way is exploring the possibilities of human potential; both are in need of freeing themselves from the captivity of their respective structures in order to face human needs based on the dynamics of today rather than the dogmas of yesterday. Each in its way wishes to address itself to the contradictions existing within societies. The question of means and ends, however, will continue to divide the religionist and the nonreligionist in their approaches to the major problems of our existence.

Is there, then, any basis for real dialogue? I raised this question often during my trips to the Balkans. The answer has been largely negative; while in daily affairs a certain level of contact and conversation links nonbelievers and ecclesiastical leaders, there is no depth dialogue between them to my knowledge in the Balkans. I found in the Orthodox Theological Academy in Sofia, for instance, portraits of Lenin and the late Patriarch Cyril hanging on the wall side by side. When I inquired if there was any dialogue symbolized by the proximity of the two portraits, the reply was negative. One churchman said, "Neither side desires dialogue, nor does either of us need it." This has been the prevailing mood in all the Orthodox churches in the Balkans. There are, of course, liaison offices in both the church and government to handle matters of mutual interest. However, there are not as yet, any depth encounters between Marxists and Christians at the point of understanding one another's presuppositions about life. Developing the latent potential of such a meaningful dialogue has for the most part been discouraged by both sides. The only real exchanges between church and state are over matters of historic interest and national political policies.

In short, the impact of Marxism and its subsequent influence upon the churches has been largely negative in the Balkans. The Marxists in the process have come to recognize that strong religious phenomena do exist at the grass-roots level. To this end, the state cooperates with religious institutions when it is expedient and discourages such cooperation when it is feasible.

The Threat of Secularization

Marxism has also broadened and extended the influence of secularization in the Balkans. Secularization as such is difficult to define, but for many in the Balkans it is identified as westernization. Some expect secular influences to have a far greater impact on furthering Orthodoxy's maturity than either nationalism or Marxism. The advent of technology with all its benefits is seen by many in the younger generation to be the beginning of a new messianism in the Balkans. This technology is associated primarily with the West; it is viewed as the new determining factor in the individual's relation to the world and his or her future place in history. In the face of this secularized technology, the ecclesiastical institutions have thus far said little.

Of course, the churches have utilized technical assistance in their programs of restoration and communication. In Bulgaria, for example, the Orthodox church employs its own technically organized team for the rebuilding of ecclesiastical buildings. There is, however, no meaningful dialogue with these technicians who are ushering in a new society. In fact, there exists a vacuum of ignorance in matters of faith among many in this secularized atmosphere. While a majority of Bulgarians, for example, believe in God, there is confusion among the populace as to what to believe in regard to this divinity. A study was made among Orthodox Bulgarians concerning their conception of God. The responses indicated varied views of God as the God-Man, as spirit, as a combination of spirit and power, but the majority seemed to view God as an undefined power. The study concluded that "belief in an undefined power is the result of the disintegration of the Christian idea of God as a complexity (person and spirit) brought about by achievements in science and technology."[9] Whether this conclusion can be rightly deduced or not depends upon other factors, but it is interesting that the study illustrates the vagueness resulting from the impact of a secular technology upon believing people. Increasing vagueness about religious beliefs can contribute significantly in weakening the position of the church as the general populace rises in its level of sophistication.

It is within this secularized dilution of Christianity that a leading Orthodox theologian in Greece, Christos Yannaris, calls for a revival of the local parish as the essential learning center for the believer.

"Only the life of the parish can give a priestly dimension to politics, a prophetic spirit to science, a philanthropic concern to economics, a sacramental character to love. Apart from the local parish all of these are but an abstraction, naive idealism, sentimental utopianism. But within the parish there is historical actualization, realistic hope, dynamic manifestation."[10] The impact of secularization, fears this Greek theologian, is so strong that the believers are in danger of losing their faith in God's future. In fact, of what value is Christian hope when technology promises to answer all human needs? Thus Professor Yannaras concludes that "we are bound to purposes so worldly that we have no place for the slightest eschatological vision."[11] Such a judgment illustrates sharply the intensity and seriousness of the impact of westernization and all its "secular benefits" upon the peoples of the Balkans.

The trend toward urbanization, another aspect of secularization, has also presented a challenge to the churches. It is not uncommon in Romania, for example, to find priests making regular calls upon people living in the growing "apartment culture" of Bucharest. But while the population shifted to the cities, the majority of the churches are still located in the countryside, small towns, and villages. Both physically and emotionally, many church leaders are oriented to a rural, nonsecularized, nonurbanized culture, even though the landscape is shifting rapidly. Unless the churches find support from the government and within their own ranks, this urbanized culture will continue to mushroom without a viable Christian presence. This is one of the great concerns facing the ecclesiastical institutions as they seek to minister in the secular cities of the Balkans.

The impact of secularization is above all a summons to the churches to address themselves to the totality of life. Under the encroaching influences of secularization, Orthodox churches can no longer afford to maintain a ghetto mentality of distance and separation. The churches cannot hope to keep themselves pure from the world; they are in the same circle of change and puzzlement as society. The churches can no longer protect their identity by isolation in secularized societies that are constantly accelerating their pace toward moderization. For instance, it has been reported that the Bible is one of the best-sellers in Yugoslavia, but the Bible read apart from the daily secular journals and newspapers will fail to generate the necessary spark for creative growth in the faith. Unfortunately, the only vehicle I discovered in the Balkans for intellectual confrontations with the current trends of a technologically oriented society was a single journal, *Theological Views,* sponsored by the Serbian Patriarchate.

The thrust of the majority of Orthodox journals in the Balkans is limited to factors of continuity in the form of theological questions; the history of churches, monasteries, and centers; aspects of Orthodox liturgical worship; devotional guides; news information; and the question of jurisdiction. Such an emphasis on continuity is needed, but it is not broad enough. Church publications by and large are dedicated to the preservation of Orthodox tradition and the identity of their respective nationalistic traditions; they completely ignore any creative, tension-filled dialogue with contemporary life undergoing secularization. This is a heavy price to pay for survival before a Marxist-secular challenge. The Orthodox churches have by and large maintained a conservative stance toward their present environment. Orthodoxy dares to announce to the modern world that what is relevant is the past, not the present. In this stance there is both weakness and strength. Orthodoxy in the Balkans presently is not in danger of succumbing to every passing mode, but at the same time her vision seems directed toward heaven while resigned to our earthly plight. Perhaps there is no other recourse for the majority of Christians in the Balkans who have miraculously kept their dignity in their struggle to secure nationalistic and religious self-identity through centuries of foreign rule.

To sum up, the maturing of Orthodoxy in the Balkans reveals in the first place that ecclesiastical institutions have profited significantly through the initial stage by the process of nationalization. The nationalization of their respective churches freed them from the dualistic Byzantine-Ottoman rule of hundreds of years to create their own life-styles.

The second major force toward maturity came through Marx-Leninism. Marxism saw the churches as obsolete keepers of the status quo, and thus took away many of their privileges. In the process the Communists uncovered a greater vitality than expected. The result has been various degrees of cooperative coexistence between church and state, oscillating between times of hostility and compromise.

The third major force furthering the process toward maturity is the threat of secularization (and westernization). It found the church largely unprepared to meet the technological society of today with its numerous by-products. The technological boom confronted an Orthodoxy largely possessed by a ghetto mentality, interested primarily in survival and identity rather than dialogue. This ghetto mentality has been nurtured in recent decades through the harsh treatment found under Communist governments. Secularization presents an even greater challenge to the churches than Marxism. Slowly the ecclesiastical institutions see the need to venture out of their enclaves and cautiously experiment with aspects of secularization. The future implications of secularization upon the churches remains to be seen, not only in the Balkans but throughout today's technopolis. A technologically oriented world has turned us into a global village where everyone's frustrations and hopes are known. The Orthodox churches in the Balkans, now come of age, might well contribute a *hopeful liturgy* to the realities of modern life in this era of village Christianity.

Not only have the Orthodox churches in the Balkans been subject to the power of secularization, but significant individuals with an Orthodox heritage have been influenced by westernization as well. One of the best known of these people is the Greek writer Nikos Kazantzakis. His own struggle with the secular forces of the twentieth century is beautifully and dramatically described in his many books. At this juncture in our search for a renewed spirituality for East and West, it is well for us to turn to the secularized spirituality of this dynamic Cretan.

7

Secularized Spirituality of Nikos Kazantzakis

The following words are engraved on Nikos Kazantzakis's tombstone in Iráklion, Crete: "I hope for nothing. I fear nothing. I am free." Behind this epitaph is the remarkable search for God by one of the better-known writers of this century.

In a letter to a friend he wrote, "The major and almost the only theme of all my work is the struggle of man with 'God': the unyielding, inextinguishable struggle of the naked worm called 'man' against the terrifying power and darkness of the forces within him and around him. The stubbornness of the struggle, the tenacity of the little spark in its fight to penetrate the age-old, boundless night and conquer it."[1] In his book *Saint Francis*, something of the intensity of his feeling is captured as Brother Leo (perhaps modeled on Kazantzakis) reports to Francis, saying, "I had been going from monastery to monastery, from village to village, wilderness to wilderness, searching for God. I did not marry, did not have children, because I was searching for God. I would hold a slice of bread in one hand and a fistful of olives in the other, and though I was famished, I always forgot to eat, because I was searching for God."[2] Kazantzakis's unfolding pilgrimage and struggle and the outcome are the substance of this chapter.

The Maverick Believer

Kazantzakis's epic poem *The Odyssey: A Modern Sequel* provides the essential index to his pilgrimage. Within *The Odyssey* a host of personages make an impact on Kazantzakis's thinking, from Homer to Zorba, including Dante, Shakespeare, Nietzsche, Moses, Mohammed, Genghis

Khan, Lenin, Theresa of Jesus, Saint Francis, Cervantes, Leonardo, El Greco, William James, Henri-Louis Bergson, Buddha, and Christ. He at times referred to these persons as the "bodyguards of the Odyssey," a pilgrimage that began with the rising of the sun and ended with its final setting at his death. Significantly, his epic poem begins and ends with an invocation to the sun.[3] "The sun symbolizes godhead, the ultimate purified spirit, for the central theme is the unceasing struggle which rages in animate and inanimate matter to burn away and cast off more and more of its dross until the rarefied spirit is gradually liberated and ascends toward its symbolical goal."[4] In short, the sun itself is a metaphor—a lasting statement of the transmutation of all persons and material into flame, light, and spirit.

Under the protection and warmth of the Grecian sun he loved, Kazantzakis was dedicated to choosing some great human spirit and studying it until he absorbed that spirit into his soul; then he moved on to someone else. He regarded his writings as a series of confessions on his journey to find God. He wrote in a letter, "Once again, I'm seated before the desk of my martyrdom and my joy, holding my pen, writing. I saw beautiful things in Italy and was very happy. I did a great deal of thinking, and in Assisi I lived once more with the great martyr and hero whom I love so much, Saint Francis. And now I'm gripped by a desire to write a book about him. Will I write it? I don't know yet. I'm waiting for a sign, and then I'll begin. Always, as you know, the struggle within me between man and God, between substance and spirit, is the stable leitmotif of my life and work."[5] His biographer, Professor Pandelis Prevelakis, comments that he knows of no nontheological text in which the word "God" recurs as often as it does in the writings of Kazantzakis. The major sources for his theological understandings and development of his concept of God are Christ, Buddha, Nietzsche, and Lenin.

His intellectual and emotional struggle with each of those four figures enables him to shape his model of God. Christ, whom he greatly admired, held a central fascination for him, as his novels *The Greek Passion* and *The Last Temptation of Christ* vividly indicate. Christ for him was the tragic but heroic individual who overcame the last temptation that confronts humans—the temptation to substitute a nonexistent paradisiacal heaven in place of the reality of death. Christ without his resurrection is a Christ who faces up to his cross, affirms life triumphantly at death, looks fearlessly at the abyss, and takes the leap. Christ for him is the one man who throughout his life overcame all crises and temptations until the end and who revealed to all that death is the final liberation of humankind. Death is one's salvation, not to be feared or sidetracked but to be accepted as part of the human destiny. Kazantzakis sought to show that Christ is fulfilled in death; it is not necessary to look beyond it. As Jesus said to Judas in *The Last Temptation:*

> I'm sorry, Judas, my brother, Jesus said, but it is necessary.
>   I've asked you before, Rabbi—is there no other way?
>   No, Judas, my brother. I too should have liked one; I too hoped and waited for one until now—but in vain. No, there is no other way. The end of the world is here. This world, this kingdom of the Devil, will be destroyed and the kingdom of heaven will come. I shall bring it. How? By dying. There is no other way.
>   . . . no, Rabbi, I won't be able to endure!
>   You will, Judas, my brother. God will give you the strength, as much as you lack, because it is necessary—it is necessary for me to be killed and for you to betray me. We two must save the world. Help me.[6]

From Buddha, in contrast to Jesus, the most important lesson learned was to seek a savior who could "deliver mankind from salvation." The message of the Buddha is to free oneself from fear and hope by giving up desire. Kazantzakis, a man of desires, had an undying struggle with the Buddha, which left its imprint as indicated on his tombstone epitaph. The intensity of his encounter with the Buddha is seen in *Zorba the Greek,* in which he claimed that "Buddha is the last man! . . . This is his secret and terrible significance. Buddha is the 'pure soul' which has emptied itself; in him is the void, he is the Void. 'Empty your body, empty your spirit, empty your spirit, empty your heart!' he cries. Wherever he sets his foot, water no longer flows, no grass can grow, no child be born."[7] Later Kazantzakis confessed that his life and death struggle with the Buddha was a tremendous force of destruction within him. It was a duel with a great no at the end. He felt that his own salvation depended on the outcome of that duel. Kazantzakis rejected the Buddha but nevertheless felt in the latter's debt as he sharpened his perspective on reality and furthered his quest for God.

Nietzsche pointed Kazantzakis to the struggle inherent in life. The only life that is worth living, according to Nietzsche, is that which develops the strength and integrity to withstand the sufferings and circumstances of existence without fleeing into an imaginary world. "Nietzsche taught me to distrust every optimistic theory. I know that man's womanish heart has constant need of consolation, a need to which that super-shrewd sophist the mind is constantly ready to minister. I began to feel that every religion which promises to fulfill human desires is simply a refuge for the timid, and unworthy of a true man."[8] In brief, Nietzsche enabled him to develop a faith without hope, an influence evident also on Kazantzakis's tombstone.

In *Report to Greco* he wrote, "The faith most devoid of hope seemed to me not the truest, perhaps, but surely the most valorous. I considered metaphysical hope an alluring bait which true men do not condescend to nibble. I wanted whatever was most difficult, in other words most worthy of man, of the man who does not whine, entreat, or go about begging. Yes, that was what I wanted. Three cheers for Nietzsche, the murderer of God. He it was who gave me the courage to say 'That is what I want!'"[9] Thus with hope and fear placed under surveillance, Kazantzakis made strides in his ascent toward his understanding of God.

Kazantzakis was much infatuated with Lenin. Unlike Christ, Buddha, or Nietzsche, Lenin was a contemporary whose revolution was yet young and made an indelible impression upon an idealist like Kazantzakis. While he rejected the materialistic bias of communism, he regarded Lenin as a "red Christ." His description of the Russians viewing the body of Lenin is noteworthy. He wrote, "The Russian masses stared ecstatically, with the precise gaze they had employed just a few years earlier when they viewed the rosy, blond face of Jesus upon the gilded rood screens. This man was also a Christ, a red Christ. The essence was the same: humankind's eternal essence, made of hope and fear. Nothing had changed but the names."[10] The significance of Lenin was precisely the concern of the "red Christ" for justice among people.

This emphasis upon justice is stated more explicitly in *The Fratricides* by the character Father Yanaros, the leading figure in this novel about a Christlike monk caught in the fratricidal struggle of the Greek Civil War of this century. Crying within himself, the monk exclaims that "the world has no need of crucified Christs any longer, it needs fighting Christs! Take a lesson from me. Enough of fears and passions, and crucifixions; get up I say, call out for the army of angels to descend; bring justice. Enough they've spit on us, beaten us, made us wear a crown of thorns, crucified us; now it's the turn of the resurrected Christ. . . . We want the Second Coming here, here on earth, before we die. Get up, rise! And a deep sad voice came from the depths of his inner being: 'I cannot . . .'"[11] Elsewhere Lenin's teachings are referred to as the Fifth Gospel, especially directed to workers of the world to unite in the cause of justice. Explaining the revolutionary shift to Father Yanaros, the village teacher says, "We haven't changed much; we only changed the word 'Christ' to 'the people'—it's the same thing. That's what God is today, anyway—the people!"[12] Today, "the people" have risen from the dead.

This brief exposition of Kazantzakis's pilgrimage shows something of the content and the intensity of his quest for God. The above mentioned names do not, of course, exhaust Kazantzakis's list of heroes. It does, however, indicate the directions his relentless quest took. He was indeed a soul in search of himself. In poetic form, *The Odyssey: A Modern Sequel* is actually a personal theological expression of his quest, which like the sun's flame consumes and transforms the searcher.

The Necessity for Struggle

To appreciate fully Kazantzakis's pilgrimage, we should more closely examine his methodology—the dialectics of struggle that preoccupied him at each stage of his theological journey. Struggle was at the essence of his life-style, an essential ingredient in the model of God that he was fashioning. "Pain is not the only essence of our God," he remarked, "nor is hope in a future life or a life on this earth, neither joy nor victory. Every religion that holds up to worship one of these primordial aspects of God narrows our hearts and our minds. The essence of our God is STRUGGLE. Pain, joy, and hope unfold and labor within this struggle, world without end."[13] Kazantzakis believed in the necessity of struggle; to battle gives meaning to the confused forces that confront us in our existence.

The nature of this struggle was dialectical—opposites clashed as new insights sought to be born. It has been said that "the greatness of man is rooted in his contrasts: being both social and antisocial, he must escape 'conformity' in order to become a creator."[14] The battle of contrasts was woven into the very tapestry of life for Kazantzakis. He sought to synthesize the contrasting figures and teachings of Christ, Nietzsche, Bergson, Buddha, Lenin, and other great human spirits. The extent to which he succeeded unfolds in *The Odyssey: A Modern Sequel.* Instead of a synthesis, a new creation emerges—a "God" in a human collage of images.

In the process of this dialectical struggle, a growing awareness struck Kazantzakis that he would not find *the God* whom he was seeking. Nevertheless he pushed on, hoping against hope to find God. At times he felt quite lonely and solitary in his search. God increasingly for Kazantzakis and his Odysseus became identified with the primordial force that drives all people to surpass themselves. Both Kazantzakis and Odysseus are literally "hunters of God." Odysseus mocks those who seek or think they have found God and boasts that he knows the great secret:

> Some crackpots search for God, thinking perhaps he lurks
> somewhere amid the branches of the flesh and mind;
> some squander precious life, chasing the empty air;
> some, still more pigeon-brained, think they've already found him
> and work on his compassion with their begging whines
> till their minds break from too much joy or too much pain.
> But others, great brain-archers, know the secret well:
> by God is meant to hunt God through the empty air![15]

In *The Saviors of God* Kazantzakis wrote that "it is not God who will save us—it is we who will save God, by battling, by creating, and by transmitting matter into spirit. . . . Life is a crusade in the service of God. Whether we wished to or not, we set out as crusaders to free—not the Holy Sepulchre but that God buried in matter and in our souls."[16] Here we have in substance the object of his relentless pursuit to transform matter into spirit. The process of struggle itself is a form of divinization.

Kazantzakis's Eastern Orthodox background is reflected precisely at the point of divinization, or *theosis*, which is the destiny of the redeemed believer. *Theosis* was the very thing for which his soul searched from the beginning. However, he placed the concept of *theosis* within a solely anthropomorphic context that made him appear unorthodox to his Greek church. God for him was one who struggles constantly and eternally; it is the destiny of humankind to be enablers—"saviors of God." In a personal confession he noted, "All my life, I have tried to expand my mind to breaking point, in order to forge a great idea, one able to give a new meaning to life, a new meaning to death, and to console mankind."[17] This attempt to reach beyond the boundaries of limitation was for Kazantzakis a confrontation of divine dimension.

The thirst after God for Kazantzakis was actually an agonizing ascension of the soul. "My head," he said, "is like a flame eternally consuming the body. But the night wind blows to extinguish me. I am threatened in my struggle every moment. In my struggle every solid body is a danger. I walk, stumble among the flesh like a benighted wayfarer, and I cry: 'Help!'"[18] For Kazantzakis, this battle with the "Invisible One" assumed cosmic dimensions. "The struggle of the Invisible One does not involve mankind only: it involves the whole earth, the whole universe. In the wild flower and in the star the same breath courses, storms, generates. Man 'has visions' of the Invisible One that 'treads on what is visible and ascends.' Struggle is the essence of the Invisible Power. 'What is the object of this struggle?' man asks, forgetting that the Great Breath does not work within human time, place, or causality."[19] From this agonizing battle his model of God began to take spiritual shape.

Exactly what new face of God was shaping on the horizon for him? The new face of God must consist of our own flesh and blood. According to Kazantzakis, God is neither an abstract thought nor a pure figment of our mind. "He is man and woman, mortal and immortal, dung and spirit. God dances beyond the bounds of logic. He is not almighty, not all-holy, not all-wise. God is like an erotic wind shattering corporeal forms in order to pass through them. God battles without any certitude."[20] It was clear for him that God's salvation and our salvation are integrally one. There is no salvation for the one without the other. "We cannot be saved, unless he is saved. We are one. From the blind worm in the ocean's depth to the infinite arena of the Galaxy, there is one alone who is struggling and in peril: ourself. And within our small earthly breast there is one alone who is struggling and in peril: the Universe."[21] Thus we can see in outline the emerging model of Kazantzakis's God with cosmic-anthropomorphic roots. A God whose birth takes place through the dialectic necessity of struggle.

Kazantzakis's methodology reveals that he was not only a literary philosopher but a theologian incognito. As he himself indicated in a conversation with a friend, "My aim is not Art for Art's sake, but to find and express a new sense of life. . . . In order for me to attain this aim, there are three paths: (1) the path of Christ—inaccessible; (2) the path of St. Paul—the combination of Art (the Epistles) and Action, but a Christ is needed; (3) the path of Art or Philosophy."[22] Kazantzakis chose the path of philosophy and therefore never regarded anything he wrote as "perfect" from the art viewpoint. He definitely felt that his efforts transcended the limits of art.

Through the exercise of writing he would feel increasingly relieved from the battle raging within him. Yet he realized that this relief was not enough. "To attain my aim," he said, "I must make a leap. As soon as this leap is accomplished (which can only be an example of life and not one of Art and writing), I shall find the expression of my soul . . . which will probably be an action and a form of teaching rather than writing."[23] Whether one is ever capable of taking the ultimate leap is questionable. Herein lies the tragic sense of life. Acknowledging this, life for Kazantzakis was an expression of heroic tragedy. There is no doctrinaire end to the struggle. The courageously free person is one who can joyfully continue without hope of any final resolution to the struggle or of reaching the divine object of pursuit. Kazantzakis's dialectical methodology dictated an unresolved tension until the end.

Death as Ultimate Reality

At the end of everyone's pilgrimage there is death. Death is the ultimate reality behind Kazantzakis: the point at which the unresolved tension of the dialectical struggle ceases. Kazantzakis and his *Odyssey,* having challenged philosophies and gods throughout life, realize now that human existence remains without justification and that there is no final judgment awaiting us. The outlook is a form of "Dionysiac nihilism" that stops short of total nihilism. There is a definite affirmation of life in the midst of this drive to question and destroy the inadequacies of all philosophies of life and gods that we worship. These philosophies and gods must be overturned if we are to be liberated. In the process of devastating these philosophies and gods is the deep and constructive exaltation of life sensed to the point of lust in Kazantzakis's writings. To meet the tragic sense of life, he counters with a painful hunger for life. He captures his thirst for life in the novel *Freedom or Death* in a conversation between the Grandfather and the young messenger Mitros:

> "Grandfather," he said, seizing the old man's hands, "I hear that you have lived like a great oak tree. You have breathed storms, suffered, triumphed, struggled, labored for a hundred years. How has life seemed to you during those hundred years, Grandfather?"
> "Like a glass of cool water, my child," replied the old man.
> "And are you still thirsty, Grandfather?"
> The graybeard raised his hand, so that the wide sleeves of his shirt fell back and revealed the bony, furrowed arm as far as the shoulder.
> "Woe to him," he cried in a loud voice, as though he were pronouncing a curse, "woe to him who has slaked his thirst!"[24]

Death, life, and God were all organically related for Kazantzakis. "Death is that point where God touches man."[25] In a more complete context in *The Odyssey,* he wrote lyrically on the meaning of death:

> My son, I too watch Death before me night and day;
> the proudest joy which now unites us here on earth
> is that we've emptied both our hearts of gods and hope,
> yet you sink nerveless to the ground, for loneliness
> has driven you wild, and freedom cleaves your head in two.
> But I hold Death like a black banner and march on!

> When I drink water my mind cools to its deep roots,
> for I know joy is fleeting and does not return;
> I munch bread and rejoice to know that I case crumbs
> in my frail body's furnace that my soul may blaze;
> I take my joy of woman till the whole earth laughs
> and nestles sweetly in my arms, in haste to feel
> before I die, my sacred heir stir in her womb.
> Death is the salt that gives to life its tasty sting![26]

This dynamic affirmation of death in the midst of one's lust for life took on a divine thrust for Kazantzakis. In Father Yanaros's study (in *The Fratricides*) of the icon of Saint Constantine, the firewalker, he says to himself, "God is not cool water—no, He's not cool water to be drunk for refreshment; God is fire, and you must walk upon it; not only walk, but most difficult of all—you must dance on this fire. And the moment you are able to dance on it, the fire will become cool water; but until you reach that point, what a struggle, my Lord, what agony!"[27] Kazantzakis engaged here in a theological statement of the dynamics inherent in everyone's life-and-death struggle on earth. The battle for meaning is itself a divine activity. The search for God is a personification of the Divine which ultimately devours the pursuers and turns us into spirit at death.

It is from this perspective that Kazantzakis was able to attribute so many characteristics to God, for the divine is woven into all the dynamics of living from birth to death. This is why Zorba is able to say in his colorful manner that "God enjoys himself, kills, commits injustice, makes love, works, likes impossible things, just the same as I do. He eats when he pleases; takes the woman he chooses. If you see a lovely woman going by, as fresh as clear water, your heart leaps at the sight. Suddenly the ground opens and she disappears. Where does she go? Who takes her? If she's a good woman, they say: 'The devil's carried her off.' But, boss, I've said so before, and I say it again, God and the devil are one and the same thing!"[28] Zorba's "boss" also concurs: "God changes his appearance every second, Blessed is the man who can recognize him in all his disguises. At one moment he is a glass of fresh water, the next your son bouncing on your knees or an enchanting woman, or perhaps merely a morning walk."[29] The many faces of God are a view of us quenching our great thirst at different stages of our relentless search for God.

To be aware of the many faces of God raises the question whether some faces are not more authentic than others. Kazantzakis was suspicious of the faces of God supported primarily by institutional Christianity. It can be seen why he was *persona non grata* to his own Greek Orthodox Church. Listen to a young, wounded guerrilla fighter speaking to Father Yanaros in *The Fratricides:*

> "You asked me who I am; I'll tell you everything in a little while; I'm anxious to get to the point. I was deacon to a bishop; I was educated, aiming for a bishopric myself. But I saw too many things—my mind opened, I understood. The word of Christ has been degraded, His message upon earth has faded; we only follow the footprints that Satan's feet leave on the mud—Christ's words have been reversed:
>
> > Blessed are the deceivers in spirit, for theirs is the kingdom of heaven.
> > Blessed are the violent, for they shall inherit the earth.
> > Blessed are they which do hunger and thirst after injustice.
> > Blessed are the unmerciful.
> > Blessed are the impure of heart.
> > Blessed are the warmakers.
>
> These are what we call Christians today."[30]

In short, the God that was real for Kazantzakis is identified with shame, disgrace, and tears rather than happiness, glory, or comfort, which dull the senses to the need for justice and satisfy us too easily with a promise of hope in some nonexistent realm. The last temptation to be overcome is hope, according to Kazantzakis.

In his search for God, Kazantzakis became a prophet of nonhope. For him, "a world without God had no foundations, but a world without justice cannot be governed."[31] Of course, the price of justice is high; this is why everyone is always in need of mercy. To seek justice and to show mercy everyone must exercise freedom. Father Yanaros standing in the church's courtyard over his own grave triumphantly responds for Kazantzakis: "'Death, I do not fear you,' he murmured, and suddenly he felt free. What does it mean to be free? He who does not fear death is free. Father Yanaros stroked his beard, satisfied. God, he pondered, is there a greater joy than freedom from death? 'No,' he went on, 'no!'"[32] Thus we come to the last sentence of Kazantzakis's epitaph as he accepted the fact of death in the midst of his divine struggle for justice, freedom, and life.

To sum up: We have seen the pilgrimage of a well-known literary figure of this century relentlessly searching for the meaning of his existence. Kazantzakis's quest for God was actually his deep and abiding commitment to the human spirit which he came so imperfectly to designate as "God." Man or woman seen within this divine dimension is the Great Combatant in life.

The essence of God is this unceasing struggle that rages within us. God is dependent upon us. According to a note in Kazantzakis's epic poem *The Odyssey*, Odysseus "tells his troops that all adventures and all experience lead to further revelations of God, that God grows as man grows, changes with man's environment and culture, for it is man who feeds him: 'God is the monstrous shadow of death-grappling man.' God needs us, not out of love, but because we are the flesh through which he lives and grows."[33] We are personifications of God for Kazantzakis; *the search* is the arena of dialogue and struggle between the two. We are souls in search of ourselves. Our pilgrimage never ceases until death.

Kazantzakis's understanding of God is both an affirmation and a denial of traditional Christian theology. His radical affirmation of the incarnation (God coming into human flesh) is at the same time also a denial of the incarnation (transforming *all* matter into spirit). Christian theology insists on the organic oneness of flesh and spirit as witnessed in the incarnation of Jesus Christ.

Another emphasis of Kazantzakis that raises questions is his attempt to view all human activity within the boundaries of this life. Is it necessary to choose between life now and life hereafter? Can we not affirm both? Can we not enjoy the experience of freedom, and at the same time affirm both the reality of death and the promise of the resurrection? Christian theology rightfully points us to a life without boundaries.

Kazantzakis's spirituality, then, is both radically Christian (the hunger for freedom) and non-Christian (the opposition to hope). He has rightly stressed the need for *freedom* in our struggle to find meaning in life. He has taken a necessary look at the abuses of religiosity in the name of Christ and has shown a divine passion to keep life human. In this pursuit to humanize life, however, is it necessary for him to strip us of hope? Obviously, there are many false hopes, wishful dreams, and pretentious illusions that need to be destroyed. Possibly, Kazantzakis is critical mainly of those pious, introverted types of hope that ignore injustice and thereby misplace their love and concern. Biblical hope, however, taking its clue from the Incarnate One, seeks to further the intrinsic worth of everyone without respect to class, color, or sex. If Kazantzakis is pointing to a rejection of this kind of hope, he has weakened his own cause. Notwithstanding this reservation, his epitaph presents a challenge to any who seek God today.

Kazantzakis's own secularized spirituality highlights for us the boundless energy the human spirit has to expend in finding peace and inner harmony with oneself and with God. In actuality the search for an abiding spirituality transcends tradition, institution, and geography. The Spirit of God, like the winds of nature, blows as it wills and lifts us individually and collectively to new heights of spiritual esctasy and growth.

8

Beyond Icon and Pulpit: Theologizing Without Boundaries

We are living on the threshold of the twenty-first century; the year A.D. 2000 is fast approaching. The urgency for thinking in terms of tomorrow's context has motivated many to challenge and discard various cultural, political, scientific, and theological stereotypes. Our sense of continuity and our respect for the status quo have been blurred and confused. What has been true is now under fire, and what has been acceptable is now considered obsolete. What does this say to Christians, whatever their confessional leanings?

Theology and Technology

It is true that we are living in an exciting, as well as a threatening, era in which to theologize. Theologizing is the rigorous and daily exercise of relating the Word of God to the human world. The context for our theologizing must be global. Parochial theologizing is antiquated, if not demonic, in our day. We have come from an age of disputes to one of dialogue, from divergence to convergence, from polemics to irenics. We have today technological universality, if not ecclesiological catholicity. Our electronic age has created an environment that theologizing Christians cannot ignore. Within this milieu it is anachronistic to delineate sharply between Eastern and Western categories of thought and action—technology as never before has made it possible for us to see the world as a whole. Fragmented theologizing, Eastern or Western, will take us back to the boundaries that describe yesterday's world.

Theologizing often appears to be an irrelevant enterprise in this space age, with theologians who simply rehash yesterday's battles and neglect the Eternal Contemporary, the Lord of the cosmos and of universal history. The theologian today, of whatever churchly stripe, must give cognizance to the fact that we are confronted by a new world technologically—a new world of all-at-onceness. We have today a technological unity in which boundaries of time and space have literally vanished. Encounters between East and West, North and South, are commonplace today as witnessed by millions through satellite communication. We are living on a global island; to speak of encounter is to underline the state of our existence.

Technology has contributed significantly in creating a *technopolis*, which in turn has created an *ecumenopolis*. The theologian's task, today and tomorrow, is to theologize within the context of this *ecumenopolis*. A simplified version is the modern kindergarten class with each child involved in some aspect of painting, building, housekeeping, climbing, reading, and so on. A visitor is struck by the many directions of interest and activity. It is this "all-at-onceness," this action in all directions at once, that our theologizing must grasp, a wholeness that comprehends and directs all sides simultaneously. The theologian must no longer be satisfied with fragmented pieces of a single heritage. This fragmentation merely pays homage to the "prince of this world" and not to the Prince of Peace who is Lord in the "world to come."

As Christians we often seem to drive into the future with our eyes nostalgically committed to the rearview mirror. It is Christians, I suspect, more than Marxists, who transform historic churches into museums. We have domesticated God into a household pet, patting the Divine on the head from time to time as the mood strikes us. Our theological anxieties today are due largely to inept efforts to meet present demands for change. Encumbered by yesterday's tools and yesterday's boundaries, we are a frustrated lot, and our ecumenism at times does not witness to our health as much as it does to our sickness and inability to accept change.

Technology rather than theology is giving guidance and aid to most Christians and non-Christians in the world. Technology has advanced more rapidly in the past fifty years than in the previous five thousand years. What has theology been doing during this intervening course of time? The lack of a satisfactory answer at this point has contributed sizably to the loss of interest of clergy and potential candidates for vocations within the church—a problem shared ecumenically by all the churches. Men and women with vision and a sense of commitment are looking for possibilities that promise reward for their use of imagination and creativity, not churches that offer a tasteless menu of caution and withdrawal in the guise of responsible Christianity.

Technology and Eschatology

Technology has created an open approach to the future. Walls and borders between nations and persons are increasingly ineffective. Technology has actually made the theological category of eschatology an immediate and current topic of concern within this age. Eschatology is much more than a stilted doctrine of last things concocted by theologians and rejected by suspicious laity; within a technological setting it is more than ever to be considered a doctrine of hope, a doctrine of the future. Eschatology connotes the future, and the future with its limitless possibilities is the aim of an advancing technology.

The technologist and the theologian are in fact working toward the same goal; precisely at this point the biblical faith has abiding relevance as it bears witness to the transcendent *eschaton*—to a timeless and spaceless order of reality. Here the technologist and the theologian are conversing in similar categories, and the former will begin to understand that the theologian, like the technologist, is also open to the future. Together they can become creative partners under the Lord of universal history and of the cosmic process, whose ways are manifest in the very forces and energies of life. It is the theologian's task to point out that it is our Lord's sovereignty over these forces and energies of life which is the true offense of the gospel in a post-Constantine, postmodern era. The problem today is that it is not God's sovereignty, but our parochial stubbornness as Christians stuck in yesterday's world, which has become the present offense in place of the gospel.[1]

It is from this ecumenically and universally shared hope in the *eschaton* that theology and technology can together look with confidence, anticipation, and openness toward the future. It is really from the viewpoint of the end of history that our present endeavors will be evaluated. Loss of this eschatological perspective can lead theologians to premature despair and technologists to a false optimism. An eschatological perspective addresses our essential nature as persons, namely, that we are anticipatory creatures whose very breath is a gift, a grace from the Creator.

The phrase "gift of grace" is the believer's way of expressing hope in the future. The believer knows by faith that nothing is permanent; everything passes away. Only hope in the *eschaton* abides. The Christian is open to the future; each day is a part of an earthly pilgrimage to discover God's grace. Each follower thrives in the security of this hope, thereby transcending the insecurities of the moment. One thus learns daily to "hang loose," to keep moving within the landscape of the *eschaton.*

Christians have not always maintained this vision of hope. Many of our church structures and edifices testify to our dated handling of the gospel. Today we are abandoning these structures but are moving without direction in a dangerous superficial search for relevance. Our structures in some cases have mortgaged us into the future, increasing our immobility and damaging our organic life as the *ecclesia* of God. Ecumenically, various churches at times appear more committed to real estate than to the journey of faith. Have we forgotten that we serve a pilgrim God? It appears that not only are our assets frozen but also our means of conveying the gospel in each new situation. The consequence is restlessness among those who have remained within the church as well as among those who have left. Church drop-outs are an increasing tribe in our day.

Restlessness is a common condition for humans in the midst of rapid change. Not only in the church but everywhere, we can observe this frustration. Some denounce this spirit of unrest as dangerous, but the technologist in each of us empathizes with the unrest for it encourages innovation and experimentation. Restlessness from the theologian's standpoint is a manifestation of our eschatological nature as persons organized in churches. As we probe into ourselves, we realize that neither new computer gadgets nor excellent church programs will satisfy our restless drives. There resides deep within our theological psyche a desire to be somewhere, to possess something or someone.

For many this restlessness is found in the routine of home life. I recall, for example, an impatient young son approaching me one afternoon with, "Daddy, I want something." "What do you want?" "I don't know!" After some minutes we finally settled, I thought, upon one of his games. Within two minutes his reaction was "I hate it." Isn't this our common plight, shared by theologians, technologists, and others? We want something, we want it now, only to hate it a moment later as we push on restlessly. It is the theologian's opportunity to furnish leadership and to work creatively in bearing witness to the pilgrim God whose *eschaton* is our hope and our destiny.

To say that Jesus Christ is our hope and our destiny is to say that Christianity is eschatology. The essence of the Christian faith is hope that looks to the future and moves forward, transforming and revolutionizing the present. As theologian Jurgen Moltmann in his book *Theology of Hope* has aptly stated,

> The eschatological is not one element of Christianity, but it is the medium of Christian faith as such, the key in which everything in it is set, the glow that suffuses everything here in the dawn of an expected new day. For Christian faith lives from the raising of the crucified Christ, and strains after the promises of the universal future of Christ. Eschatology is the passionate suffering and passionate longing kindled by the Messiah. Hence eschatology cannot really be only a part of Christian doctrine. Rather, the eschatological outlook is characteristic of all Christian proclamation, of every Christian existence and of the whole Church.[2]

It is only as we are able to focus clearly upon this eschatological emphasis seen in the biblical faith that we will have a saving word for the restlessness in society and in the individual, who knows in the intimacy of his or her heart that we are all eschatological beings—persons who long for a future with meaning and life.

For the Christian, the question of the future is organically linked with Jesus Christ. The task of Christian theology is to determine if there is a future with Christ. Ultimately the resolution of the question itself is beyond empirical verification. For the present the believer lives on the history of promise witnessed to in the biblical story (*Heilsgeschichte*). The fulfillment of the promise has not yet been fully consummated. For the time being the Christian lives in hope and in doubt—the resulting tension creates a living faith in some and despair in others. Many secular-oriented Christians have long since ceased to attribute any future to God, while Marxist and secular humanists have organized their lives toward a future without God. The present with its affirmation and contradiction is actually the very source by which a Christian view of hope is sustained. Blaise Pascal recognized this tension: "The present is never our end. The past and the present are our means; the future alone is our end. So we never live, but we hope to live; and, as we are always preparing to be happy, it is inevitable we should never be so."[3]

To hope, then, is to be human, and to hope in Jesus Christ is to be Christian. The absence of hope is despair; in its absence we tend to give too much credence to the status quo. It is the very nature of hope not to take things as they are, but to see the possibilities of change. Herein lies a spirit of kinship between the theologizing believer and the technologist. Thus, the Christian message of hope centered in the death and resurrection of Jesus Christ speaks out and gives strength throughout all the seasons of life, Moltmann says, "because in the promises of God it can see a future also for the transient, the dying and the dead. That is why it can be said that living without hope is like no longer living. Hell is hopelessness, and it is not for nothing that at the entrance to Dante's hell there stand the words: 'Abandon hope, all ye who enter here.'"[4] Christianity is eschatology personified in Jesus Christ; he is the enacter of the *eschaton*. Through him eschatology implies a theology of hope, a theology of openness to the future, a theology without boundaries, which witnesses to the God of the future whose power has been revealed in the Word made flesh.

The Triangle of Hope

As tomorrow's Christians we must articulate this eschatological dimension within our churches as well as within our cities. Each of us stands within an ecclesiastical tradition that we call "home." Our church home holds memories of warmth, security, and communal bonds of support. Some of us in retrospect know that we belong to several homes; we are the ecumenically displaced of this century. We live beyond icon and pulpit. We have changed churches more than once in our restless search for warmth, security, and fellowship. Protestants more than Orthodox and Roman Catholics have shown greater mobility at this point and perhaps more consciously question their "home" and their Christian upbringing. Orthodox and Roman Catholics, however, also have of late an increasing number among their members crossing confessional lines to seek openness to the future while realistically realizing that their own respective traditions cannot be bypassed, that their own time to influence change is rapidly dwindling, and that they have a responsibility to their children to transmit, however imperfectly, the truth which they are pursuing. Within this matrix of churches and their encounters, there is hope.

The triangle of hope consists in uniting creatively the dimensions of tradition, time, and truth, even as they are already united in Jesus Christ who is tradition, time, and truth personified.

The first component of the triangle of hope, tradition, refers preeminently to Jesus Christ. Tradition was embodied in the Word made flesh and has been transmitted through apostolic witness, sacraments, scripture, councils, and in the ecclesiastical traditions of our several churches. A fresh look at the sources witnessing to tradition has already corrected numerous misunderstandings.

Protestants took the initiative in the nineteenth century with a critical historical view of the sources of scripture, and investigations continue as evidenced in the hermeneutical activities of the post-Bultmannians and others. Roman Catholics in the second half of the twentieth century have also shown remarkable zeal in a critical evaluation of the sources of their ecclesiastical tradition, as witnessed in the documents of Vatican II, although there are also current Vatican leaders who feel this assessment of sources has gone too far. Orthodoxy has shown its concern for Christian renewal in one of the earliest ecumenical documents, the now famous Patriarchal Encyclical calling for a Pan-Christian Council in 1920, and then again at the Pan-Orthodox conference held at Rhodes and Addis Ababa by the Chalcedonians and non-Chalcedonians respectively.

Actually Orthodoxy has yet to undertake an extensive critical examination of the sources of its tradition as attempted by Protestants and Roman Catholics. Orthodoxy may feel that such a step is neither advisable nor necessary, but the pressures of today's ecumenicity, where nothing is hidden, require a critical evaluation of sources if dialogue is to gain greater depth. Furthermore, the educated laity within parishes, even more than pressures from without, will force such evaluations. Orthodoxy can no longer advocate an apostolic and patristic theology of holiness and God-like living without critically discerning the theologizing spirit of the Fathers for the present. Let there be no misunderstanding: Orthodoxy is commended for its stress upon continuity of the church, but that is Orthodoxy's weakness as well. Tomorrow's believers are entitled to know what the theologies of the councils and of Athanasius, Irenaeus, and the Gregories convey to our day. This is a challenge to Orthodoxy to be more incarnational and critical of its own theologizing.

Today we are more aware than ever that each ecclesiastical tradition has written and followed its rendition of the "Gospel According to Jesus Christ." Thus we have the gospel according to the Orthodox, Roman Catholics, and Protestants. Ecclesiastically we have created a synoptic exposition of the tradition personified in Jesus Christ. Each of the traditions, "gospel according to . . . ," highlights the mystery and glory of the Word made flesh. We are not so naive as to think that the sum of these ecclesiastical traditions is equal to *the* tradition. Tradition personified in Jesus Christ is greater than our grasp of him in our respective traditions. Such a statement may not please the Orthodox, Roman Catholics, or even many Protestants, but from the realistic viewpoint of the *eschaton* to claim any more would be presumptuous for any household of faith. We need a more relentless search into one another's ecclesiological heritage, asking embarrassing but honest questions of one another.

We must ask these difficult questions, for all the traditions share in many of the same problems. Even as the patristic period was creative in their formulations, so must we be for our day. We can no longer hide our "soiled ecclesiastical linen" from one another. Our backyards are exposed; our sorrows as well as our joys are known. Whatever affects one household affects the other households as well. In an *ecumenopolis* there are no secrets, no triumphs, no tragedies that do not concern all of us. Christ himself calls us from our confessional caves and invites us to revamp our strategies from defense to offense, as we acknowledge one another's uniqueness and contribution in fulfilling the Christian mission and shortening the shadows surrounding his *eschaton*. Let us stride confidently together into the future.

For too long now, Orthodox, Roman Catholics, and Protestants have created idols of their respective traditions. The tragic but inevitable admission is that each sees its own tradition as faithful while its neighbor's needs reform. At least it is no longer fashionable to pass judgments upon others with finality. An eschatological perspective will humble and enliven our theologizing. Inquisitions, anathemas, and proselytism are largely passé today; tomorrow, such terms as heresy, apostasy, and infallibility will become anachronisms also. The theme of a cooperative Christian mission in the *oikoumene* is reconciliation rather than rejection.

Our Christian mission of reconciliation demands united action by us all as churches and as persons. Reconciliation is biblical and cosmic in its demands. In practice, the confessional stance of our respective traditions in their parochial settings has been "isms," ideologies that have lost the *evangel* and the eschatological note of judgment and mercy. Tomorrow's theologizing must take bolder steps, lest we become satisfied with superficial advances that resist actual change or ape culture rather than take the initiative and reshape culture in the name of Jesus Christ.

Second, within the triangle of hope, let us witness to Jesus Christ as the Alpha and the Omega. He is the personification not only of tradition but also of time. This awareness will alter our views of ecclesiastical traditions, which are products of *time*. Church traditions as they bear light to *the* tradition, in the Word become flesh, are subject to the passing of time and transmission. Therefore the theologizing process will always be hermeneutical in nature; to theologize is to interpret, and all interpretations take place in time.

Time beckons us to write new creeds. This is true, and tomorrow's theologizing must continue to demythologize and dehellenize the concepts expressed in earlier creeds. However, we cannot discard our past; we do have, for example, in the Nicene Creed an important ecumenical basis that can creatively instruct us for the future benefit of all.[5] The Nicene Creed can serve as a useful model of anticipated universality and catholicity in the midst of today's technological unity. It seems far wiser to proceed from a proven model of the past into the future than to begin with the false premise that we can theologize without acknowledging our past. Furthermore, the Nicene Creed can also serve as an important catalyst in reconciling Eastern and Western traditions.

Did the West's addition of the *filioque* clause to the Nicene Creed increase or detract from the church's understanding of the triune God? The original version of the creed read that the Holy Spirit "proceedeth from the Father" only; the later Western version said that the Holy Spirit "proceedeth from the Father and the Son (*filioque*)." Both formulas within their historical contexts no doubt sought to defend the doctrine of the trinity, but in reality became stumbling blocks of the vested interests of each's ecclesiology. Pneumatology, like eschatology, has too often been neglected for ecclesiological considerations that were uncharitably engineered by forces within the respective churches. No ecclesiastical tradition from the viewpoint of time stands pure before God's judgment seat. All are in need of confession, cleansing, and reexamination of their past with reconciliation as the goal. From such a framework, today the omission of the *filioque* might be acceptable, or a mutually agreeable rephrasing might keep intact the church's faith in the triune God and at the same time enable all Christians to share in a common pneumatology.

Such a common doctrine of the Holy Spirit will not revitalize the churches overnight, but it would remove a historic barrier that has frozen positions for too long. The lack of a common pneumatology is essentially a concession to the demonic in our midst. A commonly confessed pneumatology will enable the Holy Spirit to break out of imprisoned ecclesiastical battlelines of the past and once again, in accord with the apostles, reign as the Universal Bishop of the churches. From a common pneumatology, we can be more open to the future and to the *eschaton*.

Those of us within the triangle of hope must give our attention not only to tradition and time, but also to the third component, truth. Truth is personified in Jesus Christ, and the spirit of truth will lead us to him. Christian unity in tomorrow's theologizing must avoid seeking a unity of pragmatic purposes; it must aim at unity in pursuit of truth. We have long equated our respective traditions as being synonymous with the truth. From the perspective of the *eschaton,* our respective church traditions can only reach approximations of the truth. *The* theology of truth has been revealed to us in Jesus Christ; ecclesiastically this truth has literally been within human grasp (the Word of Truth became flesh), but experience has shown that the truth has actually escaped our grasp and total comprehension. There is a hiddenness or *mysterion* to God's revelation. This factor has caused consternation not only for the Jews and the Greeks in the New Testament, but also for Orthodox, Protestants, and Roman Catholics in their dogmatic claims for faithfulness to the truth. The question of faithful witness to the truth in the spirit of the apostles cannot be resolved here; there is no easy unraveling of the dogmas or creeds for a quick solution or verification of faithfulness. The issues of orders, eucharistic worship, and mutual recognition of one another as ecclesiastical entities without reservation continue to be sources of division.[6] There is no formula for instant unity; such a formula probably does not exist apart from the fulfillment of the end time. We must be realistic and not succumb to ecumenical impatience and discouragement as we work in and through the Holy Spirit toward the vision of one church acting in harmony within the world.

In the meantime, let us admit that Orthodox and Roman Catholics will continue to suspect the ecclesiastical reality of Protestants. Secular ecumenism, while quite helpful and popular, will do no more than relieve some pressure and frustration among the faith and order issues that divide Christians. Theological divisions will not disappear through social acts of good will, however necessary the latter are in improving the attitudes toward a more meaningful dialogue.

Cooperative acts of prayer, united programs, and an endless number of "coffee-cup communions" will go far in helping us to discover the authenticity of one another's witness, but nothing more will happen unless we are willing to pursue a theological attitude that desires truth and will in time enable us to transcend our traditions and parochial ecclesiologies. On the day of truth we will fully recognize one another as individuals within the same Christian household. Terms like "separated brethren," "schismatics," or "heretics" will no longer exist, but only the acknowledgment that the gospels according to our respective traditions are all potentially valid and complementary witnesses to him who is the tradition, the time, and the truth personified. Such a recognition will not be possible if we persist in anchoring ourselves to past heritages and conduct uncritical monologues in the present day, thereby failing to hear the Spirit's message to us through our ecclesiastical neighbors. Standing within the triangle of hope, such openness may develop united Christians of tomorrow who will be *truly orthodox, truly catholic,* and *truly reformed* as they discover the authentic notes of their respective identities, as did the early witnesses John, Peter, Paul, Martha, Mary, and others.[7]

Unity via Celebration

During the transition period en route to tomorrow's theology and the final fulfillment of the *eschaton,* we will need a working spirituality of affirmation or celebration, lest we die in the desert caused by our divisions. The marks of affirmation widely acknowledged and biblically rooted are the celebrated events of baptism, Easter, and Pentecost.

The sacrament of baptism enjoys mutual acceptance among the churches. There is an ecclesiastical unity already in baptism. The methods and practices of baptism differ in the churches, but the intent is shared by all the churches. Baptism is the message of repentance, renewal, and union with Jesus Christ. Whether proclaimed in a sermon or in the liturgy, baptism is the celebration of new life in Christ and inclusion within the community. The validity of each tradition's baptism is widely acknowledged by other churches today. The basic vow taken by the adult, or by the parent in behalf of the infant, is an identification of the believer's life with Jesus Christ and one's basic ordination into the royal priesthood—into the *laos,* the people of God. Baptism not only gives the individual identity but initiates the believer into a lifetime mission to proclaim the new life in Christ, whatever one's secular vocation.

Perhaps the future may promise a common service of baptism, as well as regular services of baptismal reaffirmation. Services of confirmation (chrismation in Orthodoxy) already seek this end, but baptism is a universally more acceptable sign among Christians; its strong biblical precedent makes it an important means by which tomorrow's Christians may make a common affirmation. Perhaps a mutually acknowledged baptism, rather than the Eucharist, will emphasize our common mission to the world.

The second event of celebration is that of Easter. Easter signifies the resurrection and the fulfillment of new life begun in baptism. Orthodoxy in its long history of martyrdom can lead the procession of tomorrow's Christians in an "Easter parade," not down fashionable Fifth Avenue, but within the cemeteries and neighborhoods of poverty throughout the world praising in unison with Protestants and Roman Catholics the Christ who is risen, indeed! Easter enables our worship to be one of doxology.[8]

Doxology—thanksgiving—is in the final analysis the basic motivation behind authentic worship. Tomorrow's Christians will, we hope, gather in their churches primarily for doxology, instead of the secondary psychological and sociological considerations that preoccupy them unduly today. Easter is a sign for Christians to celebrate; their burdens are never so great that there does not loom the possibility of a new dawn. The Light of the world does reign; the children of darkness will not have the last word; therefore rejoice, for our witness is not in vain.

A third event to celebrate together is Pentecost. Pentecost points to the *eschaton,* an *eschaton* that has happily occurred in the Christ event, but is not yet consummated. Pentecost is the promise that we will be given power in our theologizing to discover new creeds and confessions as the Christians of tomorrow. Without Pentecost we are powerless, and our liturgies and sermons are meaningless verbiage. Because we do celebrate the Spirit of Pentecost together, there is hope that in the near future we will realize another Pentecost embodied in a truly Pan-Christian Council representing the *koinonia of churches,* where significant theological agreements and understandings may be reached to enable the Eucharist and the *agape* to be celebrated as a banquet of unity presided over by the Lord of history.

At the same time, Pentecost reminds us that our expectations for tomorrow may be completely other than our findings. Pentecost prevents human manipulation, warns us against theological forecasting that expresses more of the human spirit than the Holy Spirit. Pentecost is a sign of surprise and testifies that the last word belongs to God, not ourselves. Through the celebration and power of Pentecost, men and women have become saints and missionaries within the churches. It should not surprise us to hear that the communion of saints already enjoys an ecumenicity beyond our comprehension. Pentecost, along with baptism and Easter, is an ecumenical event that can be shared in celebration by Christians as a sign of hope in our pilgrimage toward mission and unity.

Our pilgrimage, in fact, has already traveled some distance: Christians have moved from the dialectics of the past to the dialogues of the present. It is my hope that tomorrow's believers may enter into an era of *cooperative didactics*—listening, learning, theologizing, and working together as we seek to meet the pressing needs of a world whose greatest dilemma is the rapid acceleration of problems. Such a world is in need of a spirit of openness, a spirituality without boundaries.[9]

To sum up: Technological universality challenges Christians to realize theological and spiritual catholicity, with believers of all traditions working in creative tension and using their heritages as guideposts rather than as fences. The call is clear for Christians of tomorrow: There is no East nor West, no North nor South, but a unique community of churches living within a triangle of hope in pursuit of God, who has already been revealed as the Alpha and Omega, the way, the truth, and the life. This is the only tradition worth pursuing spiritually and individually as we approach the end of history before the divine seat of One who came not to condemn, but to save us.

APPENDIX

Eastern Confession of the Christian Faith

(An English Translation)*

In the name of the Father and of the Son
and of the Holy Ghost

Cyril, Patriarch of Constantinople, publishes this brief Confession for the benefit of those who inquire about the faith and the religion of the Greeks, that is of the Eastern Church, in witness to God and to men and with a sincere conscience without any dissimulation.

Chapter 1. We believe in one God, true, Almighty, and in three persons, Father, Son, and Holy Ghost; the Father unbegotten, the Son begotten of the Father before the world, consubstantial with the Father; the Holy Ghost proceeding from the Father by the Son, having the same essence with the Father and the Son. We call these three persons in one essence the Holy Trinity, ever to be blessed, glorified, and worshiped by every creature.

Chapter 2. We believe the Holy Scripture to be given by God, to have no other author but the Holy Ghost. This we ought undoubtedly to believe, for it is written. We have a more sure word of prophecy, to which ye do well to take heed, as to a light shining in a dark place. We believe the authority of the Holy Scripture to be above the authority of the Church. To be taught by the Holy Ghost is a far different thing from being taught by a man; for a man may through ignorance err, deceive and be deceived, but the word of God neither deceiveth nor is deceived, nor can err, and is infallible and has eternal authority.

*From George A. Hadjiantoniou, *Protestant Patriarch: The Life of Cyril Lucaris* (Richmond: John Knox Press, 1961), pp. 141–145.

Chapter 3. We believe that the most merciful God hath predestinated His elect unto glory before the beginning of the world, without any respect unto their works and that there was no other impulsive cause to this election, but only the good will and mercy of God. In like manner before the world was made, He hath rejected whom He would, of which act of reprobation, if you consider the absolute dealing of God, His will is the cause; but if you look upon the laws and principles of good order, which God's providence is making use of in the government of the world, His justice is the cause, for God is merciful and just.

Chapter 4. We believe that one God in Trinity, the Father, Son, and Holy Ghost, to be the Creator of all things visible and invisible. Invisible things we call the angels, visible things we call the heavens and all things under them. And because the Creator is good by nature, He hath created all things good, and He cannot do any evil; and if there be any evil, it proceedeth either from the Devil or from man. For it ought to be a certain rule to us, that God is not the Author of evil, neither can sin by any just reason be imputed to Him.

Chapter 5. We believe that all things are governed by God's providence, which we ought rather to adore than to search into. Since it is beyond our capacity, neither can we truly understand the reason of it from the things themselves, in which matter we suppose it better to embrace silence in humility than to speak many things which do not edify.

Chapter 6. We believe that the first man created by God fell in Paradise, because he neglected the commandment of God and yielded to the deceitful counsel of the serpent. From thence sprung up original sin to his posterity, so that no man is born according to the flesh who does not bear this burden and feel the fruits of it in his life.

Chapter 7. We believe that Jesus Christ our Lord emptied Himself, that is He assumed man's nature into His own substance. That He was conceived by the Holy Ghost in the womb of the ever virgin Mary, was born, suffered death, was buried, and risen in glory, that He might bring salvation and glory to all believers, Whom we look for to come to judge both quick and dead.

Chapter 8. We believe that our Lord Jesus Christ sitteth on the right hand of His Father and there He maketh intercession for us, executing alone the office of a true and lawful high priest and mediator, and from thence He hath the care of His people and governeth His Church adorning and enriching her with many blessings.

Chapter 9. We believe that without faith no man can be saved. And we call faith that which justifieth in Christ Jesus, which the life and death of our Lord Jesus Christ procured, the Gospel published, and without which no man can please God.

Chapter 10. We believe that the Church, which is called catholic, containeth all true believers in Christ, those who having departed their country are in heaven and those who live on earth are yet on the way. The Head of which Church (because a mortal man by no means can be) Jesus Christ is alone, and holdeth the rudder of the government of the Church in His own hand. Because, however, there are on earth particular visible Churches, every one of them hath one chief, who is not properly to be called of that particular Church, but improperly, because he is the principal member thereof.

Chapter 11. We believe that the members of the Catholic Church are saints, chosen unto eternal life, from the number and fellowship of whom hypocrites are excluded, though in particular visible Churches tares may be found amongst the wheat.

Chapter 12. We believe that the Church on earth is sanctified and instructed by the Holy Ghost, for He is the true comforter, whom Christ sendeth from the Father to teach the truth and to expel darkness from the understanding of the faithful. For it is true and certain that the Church on earth may err, choosing falsehood instead of truth, from which error the light and doctrine of the Holy Spirit alone freeth us, not of mortal man, although by mediation of the labors of the faithful ministers of the Church this may be done.

Chapter 13. We believe that man is justified by faith and not by works. But when we say by faith, we understand the correlative or object of faith, which is the righteousness of Christ, which, as if by a hand, faith apprehends and applieth unto us for our salvation. This we say without any prejudice to good works, for truth itself teacheth us that works must not be neglected, that they are necessary means to testify to our faith and confirm our calling. But that works are sufficient for our salvation, that they can enable one to appear before the tribunal of Christ and that of their own merit they can confer salvation, human frailty witnesseth to be false; but the righteousness of Christ being applied to the penitent, doth alone justify and save the faithful.

Chapter 14. We believe that free will is dead in the unregenerate, because they can do no good thing, and whatsoever they do is sin; but in the regenerate by the grace of the Holy Spirit the will is excited and in deed worketh but not without the assistance of grace. In order, therefore, that man should be born again and do good, it is necessary that grace should go before; otherwise man is wounded having received as many wounds as that man received who going from Jerusalem down to Jericho fell into the hands of thieves, so that of himself he cannot do anything.

Chapter 15. We believe that the Evangelical Sacraments in the Church are those which the Lord hath instituted in the Gospel, and they are two; these only have been delivered unto us and He who instituted them delivered unto us no more. Furthermore, we believe that they consist of the Word and the Element, that they are the seals of the promises of God, and they do confer grace. But that the Sacrament be entire and whole, it is requisite that an earthly substance and an external action concur with the use of that element ordained by Christ our Lord and joined with a true faith, because the defect of faith prejudiceth the integrity of the Sacrament.

Chapter 16. We believe that Baptism is a Sacrament instituted by the Lord, and unless a man hath received it, he hath no communion with Christ, from whose death, burial, and glorious resurrection the whole virtue and efficacy of Baptism doth proceed; therefore, we are certain that to those who are baptized in the same form which our Lord hath commanded in the Gospel, both original and actual sins are pardoned, so that whosoever hath been washed in the name of the Father and of the Son and of the Holy Ghost are regenerate, cleansed, and justified. But concerning the repetition of it, we have no command to be rebaptized, therefore we must abstain from this indecent thing.

Chapter 17. We believe that the other Sacrament which was ordained by the Lord is that which we call Eucharist. For in the night in which the Lord offered up Himself, He took bread and blessed it and He said to the Apostles, "Take ye, eat, this is my body," and when He had taken the cup, He gave thanks and said, "Drink ye all of this, this is my blood which was shed for many; this do in remembrance of me." And Paul addeth, "For as often as ye shall eat of this bread and drink of this cup, ye do shew the Lord's death." This is the pure and lawful institution of this wonderful Sacrament, in the administration of which we profess the true and certain presence of our Lord Jesus Christ; that presence, however, which faith offereth to us, not that which the devised doctrine of transubstantiation teacheth. For we believe that the faithful do eat the body of Christ in the Supper of the Lord, not by breaking it with the teeth of the body, but by perceiving it with the sense and feeling of the soul, since the body of Christ is not that which is visible in the Sacrament, but that which faith spiritually apprehendeth and offereth to us; from whence it is true that, if we believe, we do eat and partake, if we do not believe, we are destitute of all the fruit of it. We believe, consequently, that to drink the cup in the Sacrament is to be partaker of the true blood of our Lord Jesus Christ, in the same manner as we affirmed of the body; for as the Author of it commanded concerning His body, so He did concerning His blood; which commandment ought neither to be dismembered nor maimed, according to the fancy of man's arbitrament; yea rather the institution ought to be kept as it was delivered to us. When therefore we have been partakers of the body and blood of Christ worthily and have communicated entirely, we acknowledge ourselves to be reconciled, united to our Head of the same body, with certain hope to be co-heirs in the Kingdom to come.

Chapter 18. We believe that the souls of the dead are either in blessedness or in damnation, according as every one hath done, for as soon as they move out of the body they pass either to Christ or into hell; for as a man is found at his death, so he is judged, and after this life there is neither power nor opportunity to repent; in this life there is a time of grace, they therefore who be justified here shall suffer no punishment hereafter; but they who die, being not justified, are appointed for everlasting punishment. By which it is evident that the fiction of Purgatory is not to be admitted but in the truth it is determined that every one ought to repent in this life and to obtain remission of his sins by our Lord Jesus Christ, if he will be saved. And let this be the end.

This brief Confession of ours we conjecture will be a sign spoken against them who are pleased to slander and persecute us. But we trust in the Lord Jesus Christ and hope that He will not relinquish the cause of His faithful ones, nor let the rod of wickedness lie upon the lost of the righteous.

Dated in Constantinople in the month of March 1629.

Cyril, Patriarch of Constantinople

Notes

CHAPTER 1

1. See World Council Studies No. 5, *Councils and the Ecumenical Movement* (Geneva: World Council of Churches, 1968). See also Peter Huizing and Knut Wolf, *The Ecumenical Council—Its Significance in the Constitution of the Church* (New York: Seabury Press, 1983).

2. Faith and Order Paper no. 44, *Minutes of the Meeting of the Commission and Working Committee, 1964, Aarhus, Denmark* (Geneva: World Council of Churches, 1965), p. 41. See also pp. 70–71.

3. See John A. Mackay, *Ecumenics: The Science of the Church Universal* (New York: Prentice-Hall, 1964); W. A. Visser 't Hooft, *The Meaning of Ecumenical* (London: SCM Press, 1953); and standard lexical aids including Gerhard Kittel, *Theological Dictionary of the New Testament* (Grand Rapids: Wm. B. Eerdmans, 1964). See also William G. Rusch, *Ecumenism—A Movement Toward Church Unity* (Philadelphia: Fortress Press, 1985). Thomas Wieser, *Whither Ecumenism* (New York: World Council of Churches, 1986); Samuel Amerthom and Cyris H. S. Moon, eds., *The Teaching of Ecumenism* (New York: WCC Publications, 1987); Thomas F. Best, *Instruments of Unity* (New York: WCC Publications, 1988); and Robert S. Bilheimer, *Breakthrough: The Emergence of the Ecumenical Tradition* (New York: WCC Publications, 1989).

4. Hans J. Margull, ed., *The Councils of the Church* (Philadelphia: Fortress Press, 1966), p. 6.

5. *Ibid.*, p. 50. See for documents, J. Stevenson, ed., *Creed, Councils and Controversies* (New York: Scabury Press, 1966); Constantine N. Tsirpanlis, *Ecumenical Consensus on the Church, the Sacraments, the Ministry and Reunion* (Athens: Athens Printing Co., 1980) and *Greek Patristic Theology*, vol. 3 (Athens: Athens Printing Co., 1987).

6. Margull, ed., *The Councils*, p. 50.

7. Also referred to later as the Nicene-Constantinopolitan Creed with the added clauses on the divinity of the Holy Spirit. The Reformation also acknowledged this as an ecumenical symbol, and like the ancient church in both East and West, utilized it on Sundays. (See Margull, *The Councils*, pp. 57–58); see as well

J. N. D. Kelly, *Early Christian Doctrines*, 2nd ed. (New York: Harper & Brothers, 1960), especially Part III.

8. It is interesting to note here that the Presbyterian *Book of Common Worship* (Provisional Services, 1966) omits the *filioque* clause in the Nicene Creed in its Service for the Lord's Day (p. 25). Whether this was consciously done by the committee for the sake of unity between the East and West is not documented in the text. In any case, it is significant that the clause had been removed, but reinstated again by Presbyterians in *The Worshipbook: Services and Hymns* (Philadelphia: Westminster Press, 1972) and in their *Book of Confessions* (Second Edition, 1970) p. 1.1–3. However, the newest *Presbyterian Hymnal* (Philadelphia: Westminster/John Knox Press, 1990) places the *filioque* clause in parenthesis (p. 15).

9. The Arians, it will be recalled, advocated the absolute uniqueness and transcendence of God and thereby rejected the divinity of Jesus Christ. They believed that it was an offense to God to declare that the Son was not created.

10. Margull, ed., *The Councils*, p. 49.

11. World Council Studies No. 5, *Councils*, p. 14.

12. Margull, ed., *The Councils*, pp. 358–359.

13. World Council Studies No. 5, *Councils*, p. 15.

14. *Ibid.*, p. 16.

15. Margull, ed., *The Councils*, p. 350.

16. World Council Studies No. 5, *Councils*, p. 16. Bela Vassady points out that the whole church is steadily in the process of conciliation even without the convoking of an ecumenical council. The leading of the Holy Spirit is not bound to a council; it is a charismatic gift offered to the whole church at all times. ("Revelation, Scripture and Tradition," *Theology and Life*, vol. 9, no. 2, 1966.) I believe the church fathers at Nicaea would concur with Vassady's observation.

17. Margull, ed., *The Councils*, p. 69.

18. F. Dvornik, "Which Councils Are Ecumenical?" *Journal of Ecumenical Studies*, vol. 3, 1966 p. 315. See also, Alexander A. Bogolapov, "Which Councils Are Recognized as Ecumenical?" *St. Vladimir's Seminary Quarterly*, vol. 7, no. 2, 1963, pp. 54–72.

19. Dvornik, "Which Councils," p. 315.

20. Alexander Schmemann comments, however, that in Orthodoxy no theological definition of a council has thus far been commonly accepted. Furthermore, from an Orthodox standpoint, there is not one, but several patterns of councils, which differ in many respects substantially from one another. The basic question remains: What is a council and how does it reflect the conciliary nature of the church itself? ("Towards a Theology of Councils," *St. Vladimir's Seminary Quarterly*, vol. 6, no. 4, 1962, p. 173).

21. Dvornik, "Which Councils," p. 323.

22. *Ibid.* See also Ludvik Nemec, "Photius—Saint or Schismatic?" *Journal of Ecumenical Studies*, vol. 3, 1966, pp. 277–313.

23. Margull, ed., *The Councils*, pp. 252–253. See also H. Jedin, *A History of the Council of Trent*, I (Freiburg im Breisgau: B. Herder Book Co., 1957), especially pp. 192–218.

24. Margull, ed., *The Councils*, p. 243. See also John Calvin, *Institutes of the*

Christian Religion, Vol. II, Book IV. John Calvin made his feelings quite explicit with regard to the proper line of authority.

25. See Hans Küng, *Structures of the Church* (Nashville: Thomas Nelson & Sons, 1964); Nikos A. Nissiotis, "Orthodox Reflections on the Decree on Ecumenism," *Journal of Ecumenical Studies,* vol. 3, no. 2 (1966), pp. 329–342; and especially in regard to the Oriental and Byzantine Christians, *The Greek Orthodox Theological Review,* X, 2 (1964–65), devoted to the unofficial consultation between theologians of "Eastern Orthodox and Oriental Orthodox Churches."

26. Küng, *Structures,* p. 48.

27. *Ibid.,* p. 49.

28. World Council Studies No. 5, *Councils,* pp. 15–16.

29. Küng, *Structures,* pp. 29–30. "Naturally no one who reckons with a council by human convocation will expect mathematical unanimity; two bishops refused to affix their signatures even at the first ecumenical council" (*ibid.,* p. 32). See also William G. Rusch, *Reception: An Ecumenical Opportunity* (Geneva: Lutheran World Federation, 1988).

30. Küng, *Structures,* pp. 35–36. The quoted remarks refer to Yves Congar, "Die Konsilien in Leben der Kirche," *Una Sancta* 14 (1955), p. 162; and Tertullian, *De Paenitentia* 13, 6–7; *Corpus Christianorum seu nove Patrum collectio,* II, 1272.

31. Küng, *Structures,* p. 62.

CHAPTER 2

1. Willy Rordorf, *Sunday, the History of the Day of Rest and Worship in the Earliest Centuries of the Christian Church* (Philadelphia: Westminster Press, 1968), p. 276.

2. Michael Axkoul, "On Time and Eternity, the Nature of History According to the Greek Fathers," *St. Vladimir's Seminary Quarterly,* vol. 12, no. 2, 1968, pp. 56–77.

3. Nicolas Berdyaev, *The Meaning of History* (London: Geoffrey Bles, 1936), p. 15. See also my study *Berdyaev's Philosophy of Hope: A Contribution to Marxist-Christian Dialogue* (Minneapolis: Augsburg Publishing House, 1968).

4. Georges Florovsky, "The Predicament of the Christian Historian," in *Religion and Culture,* ed. Walter Leibrecht (New York: Harper & Brothers, 1959), p. 166.

5. H. Butterfield, *Christianity and History* (New York: Charles Scribner's Sons, 1950), p. 106.

6. Gordon D. Kaufman, *Systematic Theology: A Historicist Perspective* (New York: Harper & Row, 1968), p. 280.

7. *Ibid.*

8. Butterfield, *Christianity,* p. 107.

9. Charles B. Mitchell, "The Place of Church History" (Dubuque Theological Seminary, 1963, an installation address), p. 10.

10. Butterfield, *Christianity,* p. 107.

11. See for various philosophic and theological assumptions toward history the following work: R. G. Collingwood, *The Idea of History* (Oxford: Clarendon Press, 1951). There are, of course, many works in this area, including the studies

of Hegel, Marx, Spengler, Toynbee, Ernst Troeltsch, Tillich, Jean Danielou, Hans Urs von Balthasar, Bultmann, Arend Theodoor van Leeuwen, Louis Berkhof, Oscar Cullmann, and the Neibuhrs among others.

12. Alan Richardson strikes this balance between dogmatism and despair as he notes that, "It is in the nature of history itself to raise questions rather than to supply answers, for history is a never-ending process of reappraisal. History does not deal in conclusions that can be represented as scientifically verifiable results, and each historian who handles the weightier issues must respect the warning, 'According to your faith be it unto you.'" *History Sacred and Profane* (Philadelphia: Westminster Press, 1964), p. 272.

13. Wolfhart Pannenberg in *Theology as History*, ed. J. M. Robinson and J. B. Cobb, Jr. (New York: Harper & Row, 1967), p. 273.

14. John Meyendorff, *Orthodoxy and Catholicity* (Kansas City, Mo.: Sheed & Ward, 1965), pp. 133–134.

15. See my book *Icon and Pulpit, the Protestant-Orthodox Encounter* (Philadelphia: Westminster Press, 1968), which gives a short history of Orthodox-Protestant relations.

16. Peter Brunner, *Luther in the Twentieth Century* (Decorah, Iowa: Luther College Press, 1961), p. 25. See also John M. Headley, *Luther's View of Church History* (New Haven, Conn.: Yale University Press, 1963); John Dillenberger, *God Hidden and Revealed* (Philadelphia: Muhlenberg Press, 1953).

17. E. Harris Harbison, *Christianity and History* (Princeton N.J.: Princeton University Press, 1964), p. 279. See also Francois Wendel, *Calvin* (New York: Harper & Row, 1963); and Wilhelm Niesel, *The Theology of John Calvin* (Philadelphia: Westminster Press, 1956).

18. Harbison, *Christianity and History*, p. 282.

19. *Ibid.*, p. 288.

20. George S. Hendry, "Reconciliation, Revolution and Repentance," *The Princeton Seminary Bulletin*, Summer, 1968, p. 23. See in connection with the theology of hope, Martin E. Marty and Dean G. Peerman, eds., *New Theology No. 5* (New York: Macmillan Co., 1967); J. Moltmann, *Theology of Hope* (London: SCM Press, 1956); Dietrich Ritschl, *Memory and Hope* (New York: Macmillan Co., 1967); Georges Florovsky, "Eschatology in the Patristic Age: An Introduction," *Greek Theological Review*, Easter issue, 1956; John Marsh and Paul Verghese, "The Finality of Jesus Christ in the Age of Universal History," *The Ecumenical Review*, Vol. XV, no. 1, pp. 1–25; Jaroslav Pelikan, *The Finality of Jesus Christ in an Age of Universal History* (Atlanta: John Knox Press, 1955); H. Berkhof, "God in Nature and History," *Study Encounter*, vol. 1, no. 3, pp. 1–24; Thomas J. J. Altizer, "Word and History," *Theology Today*, October, 1965, pp. 380–393; Jurgen Moltmann, "Hope and History," *Theology Today*, October, 1968, pp. 369–386.

21. Theodore Stylianopoulos, "Historical Studies and Orthodox Theology or the Problem of History for Orthodoxy," *Greek Theological Review*, Fall, 1967, p. 394. See also John Meyendorff, "Historical Relativism and Authority in Christian Dogma," *St. Vladimir's Seminary Quarterly*, vol. 11, no. 2, 1967, pp. 73–86.

22. Stylianopoulos, "Historical Studies," p. 400.

23. James Barr, "Revelation Through History in the Old Testament and in Modern Theology," *Princeton Seminary Bulletin*, May, 1963, p. 9.

24. Rordorf, *Sunday,* pp. 280–281. Professor Rordorf also cites many patristic quotations in support of this relationship of the resurrection, baptism, the Eighth Day, and the Holy Spirit.

25. *Drafts for Sections—Uppsala 68* (Geneva: World Council of Churches, 1968), p. 7.

26. *Ibid.,* p. 13. In ecumenical discussions, re-study of our fragmented catholicity is continually taking place. This is evident in such studies as Joseph Lortz, *The Reformation, a Problem for Today* (Westminster, Md.: Newman Press, 1964); Leonard J. Swidler, ed., *The Ecumenical Vanguard* (Pittsburgh: Duquesne University Press, 1966); Heinrich Bornkamm, *The Heart of Reformation Faith* (New York: Harper & Row, 1963); George S. Hendry, *The Westminster Confession for Today* (Atlanta: John Knox Press, 1960); Joseph C. McLelland, *The Reformation and Its Significance Today* (Philadelphia: Westminster Press, 1962); and also in the *Book of Confession* of the United Presbyterian Church (Office of the General Assembly, 1967). See also sources listed in chapter 3, note 15.

27. William Schneirla, "Orthodoxy and Ecumenism," *St. Vladimir's Seminary Quarterly,* vol. 12, no. 2, 1968, pp. 87–88. See J. Gill, *The Council of Florence* (New York: Cambridge University Press, 1959), and *Personalities of the Council of Florence* (New York: Barnes & Noble, 1964).

CHAPTER 3

1. The primary sources on Cyril Lucaris are found in the *Collectanea de Cyrillo Lucario,* published in 1707 by Thomas Smith, former English chaplain at Constantinople. There is also a long letter from Cornelius van Haag, Dutch Ambassador in Constantinople during Cyril's patriarchate; *Fragmentum Vitae Cyrilli,* written by Cyril's friend Antoine Léger, Calvinist chaplain at Constantinople; and *Narratio epistolica Turbarum inter Cyrillum et Jesuitas* written by a certain C. P. For Catholic sources see A. Arnauld, *La Perpétuité de la Foi,* Parts III and IV, *Preuves authentiques de l'Union de l'Église l'Orient avec l'Église,* published in 1670. For early accounts of Cyril's career see J. H. Hottinger, *Analecta Historico-Theologica* (1652); and J. Aymon, *Monuments authentiques de la religion des Grecs et de la fausseté de plusieurs confessions de loi des Chrétiens,* published in 1708. For a collection of Cyril's surviving letters see E. Legrand, *Bibliographie Hellénique: description raisonnée des ouvrages publiés en Grec par des Grecs au 17e siècle, IV.*

Among secondary sources are the following: G. A. Hadjiantoniou, *Protestant Patriarch* (Atlanta: John Knox Press, 1961), a useful but pro-Protestant account; Gloys Pechler, *Geschichte des Protestantisme in der orientischen Kirche im XVII Jahrhundert order der Patriarch Cyrill Lukaris und seine Zeit,* Munchen, 1862; Francois Deletra, *Recherches sur la vie et l'influence de Cyrille Lucar, patriarche de Constantinople au dixseptième siècle,* Geneva, 1836; Keetje Rozemond, *Notes marginales de Cyrille Lucar dans un exemplaire du grand catéchisme de Bellarmin* (The Hague: M. Nijhoff, 1963), Richard Schlier, *Der Patriarch Kyrill Lukaris von Konstantinopel. Sein Leben und sein Glaubensbekenntnis,* Marburg, 1927; Paul Trivier, *Cyrille Lucar: sa vie et son influence (1572–1638)* (Lausanne: S. Genton, 1877), and Gunnur Hering, *Oekumenisches Patriarchet und Europaeische Politik, 1620–1638,* Wiesbaden, 1968.

Important articles on Cyril Lucaris are the following: G. Hoffman, S.J., "Patriarch Kyrillos Lukaris und die romische Kirche," *Orientalia Christiana,* 1929; J. Mihalcesco, "Les idées calvinistes du patriarche Cyrille Lucaris," *Revue d'Histoire et de Philosophie religieuses,* 1931; J. M. Hornus, "Cyrille Lucaris—À propos d'un livre récent," *Proche Orient Chrétien,* Tome XIII, 1963; R. Belmont, "Le Patriarch Cyrille Lukaris et l'Union des Églises," *Irénikon,* XV–XVI, 1938–39; G. H. Hadjiantonious, "Cyril Lucaris: The Greek Reformer," *The Reformed and Presbyterian World,* Vol. XXVI, no. 1, 1960; and Lukas Vischer, "The Legacy of Kyrill Lukaris: A Contribution to the Orthodox-Reformed Dialogue," *Mid-Stream,* vol. 25, no. 2, April, 1986, pp. 165–183.

2. Steven Runciman, *The Great Church in Captivity* (New York: Cambridge University Press, 1968), p. 261. See also E. Legrand, *Bibliographie Hellénique au 17e siècle,* IV, pp. 214–215.

3. Runciman, *The Great Church,* p. 268.

4. *Ibid.,* p. 269. Also Legrand, *Bibliographie Hellénique,* pp. 278–280.

5. Runciman, *The Great Church,* p. 269.

6. See his study, *Kyrillos Loukaris, a Struggle for Preponderance Between Catholic and Protestant Powers in the Orthodox East* (London: SPCK, 1951).

7. *Ibid.,* p. 31.

8. During my research at the University of Geneva, library officials graciously provided a photocopy of this rare handwritten manuscript.

9. Runciman, *The Great Church,* p. 283. Metropolitans normally have jurisdiction over a number of dioceses and their bishops within an extended geographical region.

10. *Ibid.,* p. 284. Also see Smith, *Collectanea,* pp. 58–59.

11. Runciman, *The Great Church,* pp. 285–286. See also J. M. Neale, *A History of the Holy Eastern Church,* Vol. II (London: Joseph Master, 1847), p. 455, for his remarks on Lucaris's death.

12. James Beaven makes this assertion about Lucaris's Calvinism in "Original Papers, Cyril Lucar, Patriarch of Constantinople," *The British Magazine,* Jan. 1, 1844 (XXV, No. III), p. 181. Professor J. N. Karmiris of the University of Athens views Lucaris's *Confession* as "a Calvinist symbolical book written under Orthodox influence, rather than an Orthodox book written under Protestant influence." Were it not (Karmiris continues) for a few touches, anyone who did not know who the author of the *Confession* was would think it was composed "by Calvin himself or by one of his circle." Karmiris reckons that only three of the eighteen chapters of the *Confession* are fully Orthodox in teaching. T. Ware, *Eustratios Argenti* (Oxford: Clarendon Press, 1964), pp. 8–9. See also J. N. Karmiris, *Orthodoxia kai Protestantismos,* Athens, 1937.

13. Runciman, *The Great Church,* pp. 280–281.

14. Timothy Ware points out that the confessions following Lucaris were also not free of outside influence. "The *Orthodox Confession* of Moghila represents the high-water mark of Latin influence upon Orthodox theology, for although Latinisms are also apparent in the *Confession* of Dositheos, they are less serious." *Eustratios,* p. 13.

15. George Hendry, "The Place and Function of the Confession of Faith in the Reformed Church," *The New Man: An Orthodox and Reformed Dialogue* (Bal-

timore: Agora Books, 1973), p. 27. See C. S. Calian, *Icon and Pulpit: The Protestant-Orthodox Encounter* (Philadelphia: Westminster Press, 1968); Edward A. Dowey, Jr., *A Commentary on the Confession of 1967 and an Introduction to the Book of Confessions* (Philadelphia: Westminster Press, 1968); Hans Küng and Jurgen Moltmann, eds., *An Ecumenical Confession of Faith?* (New York: Seabury Press, 1979); Jack L. Stotts and Jane Dempsey Douglas, eds., *To Confess the Faith Today* (Louisville, Ky.: Westminster/John Knox Press, 1990); Jack Rogers, *Presbyterian Creeds* (Philadelphia: Westminster Press, 1985); and James H. Moorhead, "Presbyterians Confess Their Faith Anew," *The Christian Century*, July 11–18, 1990, pp. 676–680.

16. Hendry, "The Place and Function," p. 27.

17. Stanley S. Harakas, "Creed and Confession in the Orthodox Church," *Journal of Ecumenical Studies*, vol. 7, no. 4, 1970, p. 783. This study, along with Professor Hendry's, was presented at the Orthodox-Reformed Consultation.

18. Quoted in Beaven, "Original Papers," XXII, 1842, p. 252. In another letter Lucaris wrote almost cynically, "If I could reform my church, I would do it willingly; but God knows that it is talking of impossibilities." *Ibid.*, XXIV, 1843, p. 625.

19. Nikos Kazantzakis, *Report to Greco* (New York: Bantam Books, 1966), p. 9. Kazantzakis, like El Greco and Lucaris, was a Cretan.

CHAPTER 4

1. See F. W. Dillistone, "Crisis of Authority," *Theology Today*, Vol. XXIV, no. 2 (July, 1967); John M. Todd, ed., *Problems of Authority* (New York: Helikon Press, 1962); Robert Clyde Johnson, *Authority in Protestant Theology* (Philadelphia: Westminster Press, 1959); George Every, *Misunderstandings Between East and West* (Atlanta: John Knox Press, 1965); Henry Chadwick and Hans von Campenhausen, *Jerusalem and Rome* (Philadelphia: Fortress Press, 1966); Jaroslav Pelikan, *Spirit Versus Structure* (New York: Harper & Row, 1968); Hans Küng, *The Church* (Kansas City, Mo.: Sheed & Ward, 1967), and *Infallible? An Inquiry* (New York: Doubleday, 1971); Alan Richardson and Wolfgang Schweitzer, eds., *Biblical Authority for Today* (Philadelphia: Westminster Press, 1951); John K. S. Reid, *The Authority of Scripture* (London: Methuen & Co., 1962); G. R. Evans, ed., *Christian Authority* (Oxford: Clarendon Press, 1988); George Tavard, "Scripture and Tradition," *Journal of Ecumenical Studies* (Dallas: Spring, 1968); Raymond E. Gibson, "A Protestant Understanding of Authority," *The Ecumenist* (September–October, 1965); John C. Bennett, "A Protestant View of Authority in the Church," *Christianity and Crisis* (March 16, 1964); Paul Verghese, "Authority in the Church," *McCormick Quarterly* (November, 1967); Nikos A. Nissiotis, "The Unity of Scripture and Tradition," *The Greek Orthodox Theological Review* (Winter, 1965–66); Gabriel Fackre, *The Christian Story: Authority—Scripture in the Church for the World* (Grand Rapids: Wm. B. Eerdmans Publishing Co., 1987).

2. See James M. Robinson and John B. Cobb, Jr., eds., *The New Hermeneutic*, Vol. II, and *Theology as History*, Vol. III (New York: Harper & Row, 1964 and 1967); Carl E. Braaten, *History and Hermeneutics* (Philadelphia: Westminster

Press, 1966); Hans Jonas, "Heidegger and Theology" (paper delivered at the Consultation on Hermeneutics [April 9, 1964, Drew University]); and Carl Michalson, *Worldly Theology, the Hermeneutical Focus of an Historical Faith* (New York: Charles Scribner's Sons, 1967).

3. To further examine the dangers of "heteronomous" authority see comments by Catholic theologian Bernard Haring, "The Encyclical Crisis," *Commonweal* (September 6, 1968), p. 588. See also Henricus Denzinger and Adolfus Schnmetzer, eds., *Enchiridion symbolorum defictionum et declarationun de rebus fedei et morum*, Edition XXXII (Freiburg im Breisgau: B. Herder Book Co., 1963).

4. In a more ecumenical spirit, but uncharacteristic of the current Vatican understanding of the magisterium, Professor Richard A. McCormick, S.J., of the University of Notre Dame, confesses with sensitivity his own pilgrimage since Vatican II on the question of authority. For him church authority does not mean competence in all areas of life; with frankness he says he has come to accept "an unembarrassed modesty about many details of human life." ("Changing My Mind About the Changeable Church," *The Christian Century*, August 8–15, 1990, p. 735.) See also the related and helpful exposition in Avery R. Dulles, S.J., *Models of Revelation* (New York: Doubleday, 1983).

5. Nicolas Berdyaev, *Freedom and the Spirit* (London: Geoffrey Bles, 1935), p. 143.

6. *Ibid.*

7. See for instance the following: Chrysostomas Konstantinidis, "Authority in the Orthodox Church," *Sobornost* (vol. 3, no. 2, 1981); Boris Bobrinskoy, "How Does the Church Remain in the Truth?" *Concilium* (148, 1981); Thomas Hopko, "Criteria of Truth in Orthodox Theology," *St. Vladimir's Theological Quarterly*, vol. 15, no. 3, 1971.

8. Bishop Kallistos of Diokleia, "The Exercise of Authority in the Orthodox Church," *Ekklesia Kai Theologia* (vol. 3, 1982) p. 942–969.

CHAPTER 5

1. See, for example, the series of articles in *Christianity and Crisis*: "Whatever Happened to Theology?" May 12, 1975, and "What Is the Task of Theology?" May 24, 1976; Thor Hall, "Does Systematic Theology Have a Future?" *The Christian Century*, March 17, 1976; Richard P. McBrien, "Whatever Happened to Theology?" *Commonweal*, April 16, 1971; O. C. Thomas, "Where Are We in Theology?" *Anglican Theological Review*, April, 1971; Schubert M. Ogden, "What Is Theology?" *The Journal of Religion*, January, 1972; Gabriel Fackre, "Sober Hope: Some Themes in Protestant Theology Today," *The Christian Century*, September 23, 1987. See also the following books: Alasdair I. C. Heron, *A Century of Protestant Theology* (Philadelphia: Westminster Press, 1980); Lonnie D. Kliever, *The Shattered Spectrum: A Survey of Contemporary Theology* (Atlanta: John Knox Press, 1981); Letty M. Russell, *Household of Freedom: Authority in Feminist Theology* (Philadelphia: Westminster Press, 1987); *Why Narrative? Readings in Narrative Theology*, ed. Stanley Hauerwas and L. Gregory Jones, (Grand Rapids: Wm. B. Eerdmans Publishing Co., 1989); Rosemary Radford Ruether, *Sexism and God Talk: Toward a Feminist Theology* (Boston: Beacon Press, 1983); Diogenes Allen,

Christian Belief in a Postmodern World (Louisville, Ky.: Westminster/John Knox Press, 1989); William C. Placher, *Unapologetic Theology* (Louisville, Ky.: Westminster/John Knox Press, 1989); Theodore W. Jennings, Jr., ed., *The Vocation of the Theologian* (Philadelphia: Fortress Press, 1985).

2. Edward Farley, *Ecclesial Man* (Philadelphia: Fortress Press, 1975), p. 6.

3. See David Tracy, "Theology as Public Discourse," *The Christian Century*, March 19, 1975; and his book *Blessed Rage for Order* (New York: Seabury Press, 1975), p. 250.

4. Mary McDermott Shideler, "The Mystic and the Theologian," *Theology Today*, October 1965, p. 262. See also Evelyn Underhill, *The Essentials of Mysticism* (New York: E. P. Dutton, 1960); and Thomas Merton, *The Seven Story Mountain* (New York: Doubleday & Co., 1970).

5. Kallistos Ware, "The Power of the Name: The Function of the Jesus Prayer," *Cross Currents*, Vol. XXIV, nos. 2–3, Summer–Fall, 1974, p. 184. For Western views of the Jesus Prayer, see Huston Smith, "The Jesus Prayer," *The Christian Century*, March 28, 1973; and Per-Olof Sjogren, *The Jesus Prayer* (London: SPCK, 1975). See also Lev Gillet, *The Jesus Prayer*, rev. ed. with foreword by Kallistos Ware (Crestwood, N.Y.: St. Vladimir's Seminary Press, 1987). The Jesus Prayer is primarily an act of love expressing an intimate and direct relationship between persons. It is much more than a technique or method; it is an opportunity to be focused solely on Jesus himself.

6. John Meyendorff, *Byzantine Theology* (Bronx, N.Y.: Fordham University Press, 1974), p. 76.

7. Kallistos Ware, "The Jesus Prayer in St. Gregory of Sinai," *Eastern Churches Review*, Vol. IV, no. 1, Spring, 1972, p. 6.

8. *Ibid.*, pp. 12–13. Meyendorff writes, "In its primitive form the 'Jesus Prayer' seems in fact to be the *Kyrie eleison* ('Lord have mercy') whose constant repetition in the Eastern liturgies goes back to the Fathers of the desert." John Meyendorff, *St. Gregory Palamas and Orthodox Spirituality* (Crestwood, N.Y.: St. Vladimir's Seminary Press, 1974), p. 24.

9. Ware, "The Jesus Prayer," p. 17.

10. Quoted in *ibid.*, pp. 14–15. See also E. Kadloubovsky and G. E. H. Palmer, eds., *Writings from the Philokalia on Prayer of the Heart* (London: Faber & Faber, 1951), pp. 84–85, for abbreviated version; also Irenee Hausherr, *La Méthode d'Oraison Hesychaste* (Rome: Pont. Institutum Orientalium Studiorum, 1927), which contains the text of Nicephorus's *Method of Holy Prayer and Attention;* and Hausherr's *Hesychasme et Prière* (Rome: Pont. Institutum Orientalium Studiorum, 1966).

11. A similar but more intricate breathing practice is found among the Sufis in connection with *dhikr* (the invocation of the name of God). For parallels between Sufism and hesychasm, see L. Gardet, "Un problème de mystique comparée: la mention du nom divin (*dhikr*) dans la mystique musulmane," *Revue Thomiste*, LII (1952), pp. 642–679, and LIII (1953), pp. 197–216. Further study is needed in this area.

12. Ware, "The Power of the Name," p. 198. See Joseph Munitz, S.J., "Prayer on Mount Athos: Reflections on Visit Made in July, 1970," *Eastern Churches Review*, Vol. III, no. 3, Spring, 1971.

13. Francois Neyet, "The Jesus Prayer," *Sobornost*, Series 6, no. 9, Summer, 1974, p. 642. See also *On the Invocation of the Name of Jesus*, by A Monk of the Eastern Church (Lev Gillet) (Oxford: S.L.G. Press, 1970); and Boris Bobrinskoy, "Nicholas Cabasilas and Hesychast Spirituality," *Sobornost*, Series 5, no. 7, Autumn, 1968.

14. Timothy Ware, *The Orthodox Church* (New York: Penguin Books, 1963), p. 75.

15. Ware, "The Jesus Prayer," pp. 8–9.

16. *Ibid.*, pp. 10–11.

17. Meyendorff, *Byzantine Theology*, p. 77. See also Meyendorff's *A Study of Gregory Palamas* (London: Faith Press, 1962). The original French edition (*Introduction à l'étude de Gregoire Palamas*, Paris: de Seuil, 1959) contains a full analysis of the published and unpublished writings of Palamas.

18. Jaroslav Pelikan, *The Spirit of Eastern Christendom (600–1700)* (Chicago: University of Chicago Press, 1974), p. 263. See also Bernard McGinn and John Meyendorff, eds., *Christian Spirituality*, Vol. I (New York: Crossroad, 1985); Louis Dupre and Don E. Saliers, eds., *Christian Spirituality*, Vol. III (New York: Crossroad, 1989).

19. Meyendorff, *Byzantine Theology*, p. 77–78. See also Georges Florovsky, "Saint Gregory Palamas and the Tradition of the Fathers," *Sobornost*, Series 4, no. 4, Winter–Spring, 1961.

20. Edward J. Ryan, "The Invocation of the Divine Name in Sinaite Spirituality," *Eastern Churches Quarterly*, Vol. XIV, nos. 4 and 5, 1961–62, pp. 296–297.

21. Edward J. Ryan, *The Way of a Pilgrim*, trans. R. M. French (London: SPCK., 1954), p. 18.

22. George A. Maloney, S.J., "The Jesus Prayer and Early Christian Spirituality," *Sobornost*, Series 5, no. 5, Summer, 1967, p. 319.

23. *Ibid.*

24. M. Basil Pennington, O.C.S.O., *Daily We Touch Him* (New York: Doubleday & Co., 1977), pp. 35–38. See also M. B. Pennington, ed., *Toward an Integrated Humanity: Thomas Merton's Journey* (Kalamazoo, Mich.: Cistercian Publications, 1988); M. B. Pennington, ed., *One Yet Two: Monastic Tradition East and West* (Kalamazoo, Mich.: Cistercian Publications, 1976); Thomas Merton, *Contemplative Prayer* (New York: Doubleday & Co., 1971); T. Merton, *New Seeds of Contemplation* (New York: A New Directions Book, 1961); Thomas Keating, O.C.S.O., et al., *Finding Grace at the Center* (Petersham, Mass.: St. Bede Publications, 1978).

25. Harvey Cox, *The Seduction of the Spirit* (New York: Simon & Schuster, 1973), p. 83.

26. *Ibid.*

27. See Adam Smith, "The Meditation Game," *The Atlantic*, October, 1975, and his book *Powers of Mind* (New York: Random House, 1975); *Science News*, vol. 109, January 24, 1976; *Science*, vol. 191, January 23, 1976, pp. 308–310; and *Science*, vol. 193, August 27, 1976, pp. 719–720. These articles from *Science News* and *Science* dispute Wallace's findings, pointing out that the meditation period during TM is not a single, unique, wakeful, hypometabolic state. Any beneficial

result derived from TM may simply be due to stages of sleep that occur during meditation or to some other feature of that process. Wallace, in response to these investigations, does concur that during the practice of TM subjects may experience several "states of consciousness," including sleep stages 1, 2, 3, and 4. Wallace also agrees with the investigations that there may be considerable variation from meditation to meditation and from meditator to meditator in the states of consciousness experienced. It almost seems that TM is actually a disciplined means of taking "cat naps" twice a day. A TM teacher during a taped interview informed me that the "scientific data" behind the TM movement needed further strengthening and that the movement was aware of it.

For additional views and perspectives on TM see David Haddon, "Transcendental Meditation Challenges the Church," *Christianity Today*, March 26 and April 9, 1976; George E. LaMore, Jr., "The Secular Selling of a Religion," *The Christian Century*, December 10, 1975; and in the same issue a *more positive* view of TM by John R. Dilley, "TM Comes to the Heartland of the Midwest." The Spiritual Counterfeits Project in Berkeley, Calif., has published "An English Translation of Transcendental Meditation's Initiatory Puja" with critical comments. See also Gordon R. Lewis, *What Everyone Should Know About Transcendental Meditation* (Ventura, Calif.: Regal Books, 1975). Of interest also are featured articles: "Meditation: The Answer to All Your Problems?" *Time*, October 13, 1975; "Getting Your Head Together," *Newsweek*, September 6, 1976; Andrew M. Greeley and William C. McCready, "Are We a Nation Of Mystics?" *The New York Times Magazine*, January 26, 1975; Richard Gibson, "The Yoga Airborne at Maharishi U. Targets Persian Gulf," *The Wall Street Journal*, October 11, 1990; and Jim Carlton, "For $1,500 a Head, Maharishi Promises Mellower Inmates," *The Wall Street Journal*, April 15, 1991.

28. In addition to the supportive testimonials and articles that can be had by writing to MIU (Fairfield, Iowa 52556-2091), see also Harold H. Bloomfield, Michael Peter Cain, Dennis T. Jaffe, in collaboration with Robert Bruce Kory, *TM—Discovering Inner Energy and Overcoming Stress* (New York: Dell Publishing Co., 1975); Jack Forem, *Transcendental Meditation, Marharishi Mahesh Yogi and the Science of Creative Intelligence* (New York: E. P. Dutton & Co., 1974); and Harold H. Bloomfield and Robert H. Kory, *Happiness, the TM Program, Psychiatry and Enlightment* (New York: Simon & Schuster, 1976).

29. See the three-part series on *The Facts on Transcendental Meditation* by Colin Campbell, Gary E. Schwartz, and Leon S. Otis, *Psychology Today*, April, 1974; and also Robert E. Ormstein, "Eastern Psychologies: The Container Vs. the Contents," *Psychology Today*, September, 1976, pp. 26–43. See also Russell Chandler, *Understanding the New Age* (Irving, Tex.: Word Publishing, 1988).

30. Sam Keen, *Beginning Without End* (New York: Harper & Row, 1975), p. 12.

31. See Henri J. M. Nouwen, *The Genesee Diary* (New York: Doubleday & Co., 1976). For further reflection on this point, see also Aelred Graham, *Contemplative Christianity* (New York: Seabury Press, 1974), Evelyn Underhill, *The Mystics of the Church* (London: James Clarke & Co., 1926); Sallie McFague TeSelle, "An Intermediary Theology: In Service of the Hearing of God's Word," *The Christian Century*, June 25, 1975; N. F. Robinson, *Monasticism in the Orthodox Churches*

(London: Cope and Fenwick, 1916, reprinted New York: AMS Press, 1971); Sergius Bulgakov, *The Orthodox Church* (London: Centenary Press, 1935); Jacques-Albert Cuttat, *The Encounter of Religions* (New York: Desclee Co., 1960); and Eberhard Bethge, *Bonhoeffer: Exile and Martyr* (New York: Seabury Press, 1975). Bonhoeffer himself wrote, "The restoration of the Church must surely depend on a new kind of monasticism, having nothing in common with the old but being a life of uncompromising adherence to the Sermon on the Mount in imitation of Christ. I believe the time has come to rally men together for this." (Quoted in Bethge, *Bonhoeffer*, p. 52, and found originally in a letter of 14.1.1935, in *Gesammelte Schriften*, Vol. III, p. 25.)

32. See Pelikan, *The Spirit*, p. 254; Tracy, "Theology as Public Discourse," p. 243; and the following: Helen Waddell, *The Desert Fathers* (Ann Arbor, Mich.: University of Michigan Press, 1957); Vladimir Lossky, *The Mystical Theology of the Eastern Church* (London: James Clarke & Co., 1957); William Johnston, ed., *The Cloud of Unknowing and the Book of Privy Counseling* (New York: Doubleday & Co., 1973); Cheslyn Jones, Geoffrey Wainwright, and Edward Yarnold, S.J., *The Study of Spirituality* (New York: Oxford University Press, 1986), pp. 235–276.

33. See Desmond Doig, *Mother Teresa: Her People and Her Work* (New York: Harper & Row, 1976); and the feature story in *Time*, December 29, 1975.

34. For further discussion of an ethic of sociospirituality see my work *Icon and Pulpit: The Protestant-Orthodox Encounter* (Philadelphia: Westminster Press, 1968), pp. 155–170.

CHAPTER 6

1. See Steven Runciman, *The Great Church in Captivity* (New York: Cambridge University Press, 1968). Also consult N. Iorga, *Byzance après Byzance* (Bucharest: L'Institut D'Betudes Byzantines, 1935) and *Byzantine Empire* (London: J. M. Dent & Co., 1907); H. W. Haussig, *A History of Byzantine Civilization* (New York: Praeger Publishers, 1971); C. U. Clark, *United Roumania* (New York: Dodd, Mead & Co., 1932); R. W. Seton-Watson, *A History of the Roumanians* (Cambridge: Cambridge University Press, 1934); K. S. Latourette, *The Nineteenth Century in Europe*, Vols. I and II (New York: Harper & Brothers, 1958); D. Attwater, *The Christian Churches of the East*, Vols. I and II (Milwaukee: Bruce Publishing Co., 1947, 1948); A. Fortescue, *The Orthodox Eastern Church* (London: Catholic Truth Society, 1920); N. Zernov, *Eastern Christendom* (New York: Putnam, 1961); and Alexander A. Pallis, *Greek Miscellany: A Collection of Essays on Medieval and Modern Greece* (Athens: published by author, 1964).

2. Runciman, *The Great Church*, p. 376.

3. *Ibid.*, p. 380.

4. For an update on the situation, see Denis R. Janz, "Rooting Out Religion: The Albanian Experiment," *The Christian Century*, July 25–August 1, 1990, pp. 700–792; and Barbara Frey, "Violations of Freedom of Religion in Albania," *Occasional Papers on Religion in Eastern Europe*, ed. Paul Mojzes, November, 1989, pp. 1–17.

5. For further discussion, see Jill Schaeffer, "Roumania: The Eighth Circle of Hell," *Perspective*, May 1990, pp. 4–6; *The Christian Century*, brief news articles in

February 28, 1990, and May 2, 1990; and Alexander F. C. Webster, "Evangelicals Vs. Orthodox in Roumania," *The Christian Century*, May 30–June 6, 1990, pp. 560–561, and "Roumanian Church Seeks to Cleanse Itself," *Ibid.*, April 3, 1991, pp. 357–358. See also *Uncertain Hope: Religion in the Soviet Union and Eastern Europe Today* (London: The British Council of Churches, 1989); Earl A. Pope, "The Contemporary Religious Situation in Romania," *Occasional Papers on Religion in Eastern Europe*, February, 1989, pp. 39–41; and Gene Preston, "Romanian Churches: Across the Years," *Christianity and Crisis*, March 18, 1991, pp. 87–89.

6. V. I. Lenin, *On Religion* (Moscow: Progress Publishers, 1965), p. 8.

7. See Peter Steinfels, "In Eastern Europe's Churches, Triumph Leads to Uncertainty," *The New York Times*, July 22, 1990.

8. Donald M. Borchert, "The Future of Religion in a Marxist Society," *The Christian Century*, September 29, 1971, pp. 1129–1133. See also my studies *Icon and Pulpit: The Protestant-Orthodox Encounter* (Philadelphia: Westminster Press, 1968) and *Berdyaev's Philosophy of Hope: A Contribution to Marxist-Christian Dialogue* (Minneapolis: Augsburg Publishing House, 1968); Miroslav Volf, "Church, State, and Society: Reflections on the Life of the Church in Contemporary Yugoslavia," *Occasional Papers on Religion in Eastern Europe*, February, 1990, pp. 1–16; Nikola Skledai, "The Marxist Philosophy of Religion in Yugoslavia with a Review of Its Contribution to the Christian-Marxist Dialogue," *Occasional Papers on Religion in Eastern Europe*, September, 1989, pp. 15–30; Arthur B. Keys, Jr., "Yugoslavs Rebuild: Faith and Society," *Christianity and Crisis*, March 18, 1991, pp. 83–87. The persistence of religion is seen even in Albania as the Albanian Orthodox Church emerges from the underground. (See comments in the *Orthodox Observer*, March, 1991, published by Greek Orthodox Archdiocese of North and South America, New York. See also Janice Broun, *Conscience and Captivity: Religion in Eastern Europe* (Washington, D.C.: Ethics and Public Policy Center, 1988).

9. K. Krustev, "Concerning the Contemporary Idea of God," *Filosofak Misul*, no. 6 (June, 1968), pp. 104–111, summed up in *Research Materials on Religion in Eastern Europe*, Vol. II, no. 8, August, 1967, p. 7. One can hope that under today's spirit of religious freedom, Bulgarians will begin to nurture and clarify their beliefs. See Janice Broun, "In Bulgaria, Religion Blossoms," *The Christian Century*, February 27, 1991, pp. 222–223.

10. Christos Yannaras, "Orthodoxy and the West," *Eastern Churches Review*, Vol. III, 3, Spring, 1971, p. 299.

11. *Ibid.*, p. 300.

CHAPTER 7

1. Helen Kazantzakis, *Nikos Kazantzakis, a Biography Based on His Letters* (New York: Simon & Schuster, 1968), p. 507. I am grateful also for the conversations held with Mrs. H. Kazantzakis during my 1970 sabbatical in Switzerland. Nikos Kazantzakis was born on December 2, 1885, and died on October 26, 1957.

2. N. Kazantzakis, *Saint Francis* (New York: Ballantine Books, 1962), p. 9.

3. See opening lines in the Prologue and Epilogue.

4. See notes by Kimon Friar in N. Kazantzakis, *The Odyssey: A Modern Sequel* (New York: Simon & Schuster, 1958), pp. 777–778.

5. H. Kazantzakis, *Nikos Kazantzakis,* p. 514.

6. N. Kazantzakis, *The Last Temptation of Christ,* (New York: Bantam Books edition, 1960), pp. 412–413. For commentary on the film based on *The Last Temptation of Christ,* see Lawrence Meredith, "The Gospel According to Kazantzakis: How Close Did Scorsese Come?" *The Christian Century,* September 14–21, 1988, pp. 799–802.

7. N. Kazantzakis, *Zorba the Greek* (New York: Ballantine Books, 1965), p. 154.

8. N. Kazantzakis, *Report to Greco* (New York: Bantam Books edition, 1965), p. 324.

9. *Ibid.,* p. 325.

10. *Ibid.,* p. 384.

11. N. Kazantzakis, *The Fratricides* (New York: Simon & Schuster, 1964), p. 250.

12. *Ibid.,* p. 180. See also Peter Bien's discussion in *Kazantzakis: Politics of the Spirit* (Princeton: Princeton University Press, 1989); and James F. Lea, *Kazantzakis: The Politics of Salvation* (Tuscaloosa: University of Alabama Press, 1979).

13. N. Kazantzakis, *The Saviors of God* (New York: Simon & Schuster, 1960), p. 92.

14. Jules Chaix-Ruy, *The Superman: From Nietzsche to Teilhard de Chardin* (Notre Dame, Ind.: University of Notre Dame Press, 1968), p. 16.

15. N. Kazantzakis, *The Odyssey,* Book XVII, p. 573, lines 1010–17.

16. N. Kazantzakis, *Saviors of God,* nos. 47 and 49, p. 106.

17. Pandelis Prevelakis, *Nikos Kazantzakis and His Odyssey* (New York: Simon & Schuster, 1961), p. 116.

18. *Ibid.,* p. 48.

19. *Ibid.*

20. *Ibid.*

21. *Ibid.*

22. H. Kazantzakis, *Nikos Kazantzakis,* p. 77.

23. *Ibid.*

24. N. Kazantzakis, *Freedom or Death* (New York: Ballantine Books, 1969), p. 370.

25. N. Kazantzakis, *The Fratricides,* p. 58.

26. N. Kazantzakis, *The Odyssey,* pp. 570–571, lines 899–912.

27. N. Kazantzakis, *The Fratricides,* p. 136.

28. N. Kazantzakis, *Zorba,* p. 263.

29. *Ibid.,* p. 234.

30. N. Kazantzakis, *The Fratricides,* p. 62.

31. *Ibid.,* p. 65.

32. *Ibid.,* p. 55.

33. N. Kazantzakis, *The Odyssey,* p. 793 (notes).

CHAPTER 8

1. See Hans Küng, *Theology for the Third Millennium: An Ecumenical View* (New York: Doubleday, 1988); John Meyendorff, *Catholicity and the Church* (Crestwood, N.Y.: St. Vladimir's Press, 1983) and *Living Tradition* (Crestwood, N.Y.: St. Vladimir's Seminary Press, 1978); George A. Lindbeck, *The Nature of Doctrine: Religion and Theology in a Post Liberal Age* (Philadelphia: Westminster Press, 1984); William C. Placher, *Unapologetic Theology: A Christian Voice in a Pluralistic Conversation* (Louisville, Ky.: Westminster/John Knox Press, 1989); Stanley S. Harakas, "Tradition in the Orthodox Tradition," paper delivered at the American Theological Society Meeting, April 20–21, 1990; and Alexander Schmemann, *Church, World, Mission: Reflections on Orthodoxy in the West* (Crestwood, N.Y.: St. Vladimir's Seminary Press, 1979); Jurgen Moltmann, *The Church in the Power of the Spirit* (New York: Harper & Row, 1977) and *Theology Today* (Wynnewood, Pa.: Trinity Press International, 1988).

2. J. Moltmann, *Theology of Hope*, English trans. (London: SCM Press, 1967), p. 16. See also Carl E. Braaten, "Toward a Theology of Hope," *Theology Today*, XXIV, 2 (1967); and C. S. Calian, *Berdyaev's Philosophy of Hope* (Minneapolis: Augsburg Publishing House, 1968).

3. Blaise Pascal, *Pensées* (London: Everyman's Library, 1954), no. 172, p. 5.

4. Moltmann, *Theology of Hope*, p. 32.

5. Geddes MacGregor, *The Nicene Creed Illumined by Modern Thought* (Grand Rapids: Wm. B. Eerdmans Publishing Co., 1980).

6. The Faith and Order Commission of the World Council of Churches has published an important booklet titled *Baptism, Eucharist, and Ministry* (Faith and Order Paper no. 111, 1982). The three agreed-upon statements in this booklet are now under discussion by the member churches; they serve as an ecumenical guideline that Christian spirituality without boundaries is not only within the realm of possibility but a cherished hope for the near future. As a long time participant in the official international dialogues between the Orthodox and Reformed churches, I must testify that the process is slow. See also Thomas F. Torrance, ed., *Theological Dialogue Between Orthodox and Reformed Churches* (Edinburgh: Scottish Academic Press, 1985); and *The Orthodox Church and the Churches of the Reformation*, Faith and Order Paper no. 76 (Geneva: World Council of Churches, 1975).

7. This book has not mentioned the issue of the ordination of women as being yet another challenge to Orthodoxy. It is certainly being discussed in Orthodox circles, as was evident in the recent Inter Orthodox Consultation, "On the Place of the Women in the Orthodox Church and the Direction of the Ordination of Women," Rhodos, Greece, October 30–November 7, 1988. See notes and comments in *St. Vladimir's Theological Quarterly*, vol. 33, 1989, pp. 392–406. See also Thomas Hopko, ed., *Women and the Priesthood (Crestwood, N.Y.: St. Vladimir's Seminary Press, 1983); and Bishop Chrysostomos, "Women in the Church: Some Current Issues in Perspective," The Greek Orthodox Theological Review*, vol. 34, no. 2, (Summer, 1989), pp. 117–125. To date, the Orthodox wish to remain faithful to the witness of tradition as understood and practiced by them. The "iconic" character of priesthood as handed down through Christ is male-oriented for the Orthodox. The role and contribution of women is highly regarded

by the Orthodox, but they do not wish to subordinate their faithfulness to tradition to the present challenges posed by feminist theology. This will be an important topic for future research and discussion in dialogue with the Orthodox.

8. See Geoffrey W. Wainwright, *Doxology: The Praise of God in Worship, Doctrine, and Life* (New York: Oxford University Press, 1980) and *The Ecumenical Moment* (Grand Rapids: Wm. B. Eerdmans Publishing Co., 1983).

9. This spirit of openness is exemplified in Anthony Ugolnik's recent work, *The Illuminating Icon* (Grand Rapids: Wm. E. Erdmans Publishing Co., 1989); and Archbishop Iakovos, *Faith for a Lifetime: A Spiritual Journey* (New York: Doubleday, 1988); Paul A. Crow, Jr., *Christian Unity: Matrix for Mission* (New York: Friendship Press, 1982); Pauline Webb, ed., *Faith and Faithfulness* (New York: World Council of Churches, 1984), *Churches in Covenant Communion: The Church of Christ Uniting* (Princeton, N.J. Consultation on Church Union, 1989).

Index

INDEX